LAWFUL OCCASIONS
THE OLD EASTERN CIRCUIT

LAWFUL
OCCASIONS
The Old Eastern Circuit

Patrick MacKenzie

THE MERCIER PRESS

THE MERCIER PRESS, 4 Bridge Street, Cork
24 Lower Abbey Street, Dublin 1

© Patrick MacKenzie 1991

ISBN 0 85342 981 2

A CIP record for this book is available from the British Library

Printed in Ireland by Colour Books Ltd.

1

1942

At six o'clock on a February morning I got onto a tram at the bottom of Ailesbury Road to catch the quarter to seven train from Westland Row. I had with me my black cloth bag, initials stitched in red, containing a tin box with a wig and gown, but no briefs. It was my first venture on Circuit and I was going to try my hand in Wicklow, some thirty miles away. The money in my pocket was less than £3, it would pay the train fare and get me some lunch for several days. I could cover my expenses if I got the most meagre brief, which of course I did not.

Just three months previously I had been called to the Bar and I soon found that I would never get anywhere by staying in the Four Courts in Dublin moping around from court to court, listening to others perform, or sitting in the Law Library devilling another's cases.

Westland Row Station was a place of little cheer on that foggy freezing morning. The train was to take one hour and three quarters to do the thirty mile run. It was powered by a furnace of damp turf and a few sticks. Clouds of steam filled the carriage, coming from a pipe which was supposed to heat the passengers.

Sitting in the compartment, awaiting the departure of the train, I can't say I felt exactly cheerful. I had the prospect of a lonely journey, to an unknown place, without even a newspaper to read. Then the door opened and in came The Ó Rathaille, who afterwards became a very good friend. A little later Seán MacBride arrived and then Vivian de Valera, and the train, with much agonising, jerked into motion.

They immediately recognised me as a newcomer to the Bar and in a most friendly way introduced themselves. Nowadays, when there are close to one thousand barristers, no one would even bother to say hello, or indeed nod. Nevertheless, I felt an outsider, notwithstanding the friendly remarks which they made from time to time.

We got to Dalkey and the darkness began to dissolve. Coming under a long tunnel, on top of which stands the house called Khyber Pass, where Parnell at one time used to live, suddenly the lovely bay of Killiney was below us. A huge red sun had just emerged from the sea. It lightened my day, I thought I had never seen such a beautiful place as this on that February morning. It was then I decided that that was where I wanted to live.

Arriving at Wicklow, at about half past nine, we had a considerable walk from the railway station to the courthouse, which stands at the southern end of the town. Behind it is the former prison. Below the courtrooms is a series of gloomy cells. Many people, particularly after the battles and uprising of 1798, were taken to the prison yard and executed on the gallows, a walk of barely fifty paces from place of condemnation to place of death. A flagged entrance hall, well suited for accentuating the freezing cold and, at that time, two arctic courtrooms, one used for criminal business, because it had a dock into which the prisoner ascended from the cells below, the other for civil business with a more congenial atmosphere, comprised the complex.

The old legal buildings in Ireland have been a source of pleasure and interest to me. Mostly they are well constructed and of architectural distinction. The principal courtroom in a country town is characterised by a high balcony where the Grand Jury used to sit and to whom a Clerk of the Peace handed up the documents on a cleft stick, this balcony sometimes being sixteen feet from ground level. The decision of these gentlemen was handed down in the same manner. Usually there was a high gallery for the accommodation of the general public, and a Jury Box, mostly on the judge's right hand side. Witnesses gave their evidence sitting on a chair placed on a large table facing the judge, around which, usually in half moon shape, were seats for counsel, behind again, tier upon tier were places for attorneys, witnesses and others involved in the proceedings. Modernisation by officials has sometimes produced deplorable results.

The Wicklow courthouse also had two rooms for the legal profession, one for solicitors and one for barristers, both equally dirty and ill-furnished. Heating came from a fireplace upon which two damp sods of turf smouldered. The courtrooms, however, were beautiful. Although then decayed, they have now been well restored.

Judge Michael Comyn who presided over the Eastern Circuit at that time, was the most popular and most humane of all the Circuit judges. He was a stout old man with battered wig, and across his large corporation was a gleaming gold watch chain. From time to time he took snuff with a loud sniff and a blow of his nose. All cases had a great fascination for him. He frequently made remarks after hearing an opening statement.

'Oh, I'll hear this case, I'll try this case, I'll get to the bottom of it if I have to stay here all night.'

And he'd put his wig back.

'Put up your witnesses now.'

Art O'Connor, who was one of the leaders at that time on the Circuit, introducing one case said:

'My client, m'Lord, is a widow.'

'You don't say. That's all right, Mr O'Connor', said the judge. 'She's a widow, is she? We'll do right by the widow.'

Afterwards, instinctively, the Bar felt that before him widows had a sort of divine right, and this persisted long after his regretted retirement. Art to me looked like an old man of the judge's generation. Like him he had a large comfortable corporation. Getting on to his feet to open his case, he used to pull up his stomach and place it on the table. The judge always looked down and said, 'Take your time Mr O'Connor, settle yourself comfortably.'

Seventy years is the retirement age for a Circuit Court Judge. To me Michael looked as old as Methuselah. That first morning in Wicklow I was told that he was in fact well beyond seventy years and should have retired long ago. He seemed to me a monument of benevolent antiquity — that is on most occasions. It was said that his birth was never registered, a civil act which was often forgotten about in rural Ireland. The Department of Justice were constantly querying him, suggesting that he ought to retire. As his age could never be proved, he maintained that he had years ahead of him.

With a bright idea, a civil servant departed for the birthplace of the learned judge somewhere near Ennis in the county of Clare to inspect the parish register, thereby hoping at least to establish the date of his baptism, which presumably was shortly after his birth. In those days, children were christened within a week or so of their coming into the world. When he was shown the register by the parish clerk, after chasing around from pub to pub to find that worthy, on opening the register, the book in which births, deaths and marriages were registered, a particular page was torn out of that section where, the civil servant had calculated, the old man's date of baptism would have been inserted with the name of the celebrant. The parish clerk was bemused: 'I don't know how that happened', he said. 'All the other pages is there. But sure no one ever looks that far back.'

The order of business in the Circuit Court involved a variety of cases. Firstly, criminal trials took place, then District Court appeals, thereafter civil business occupied the time, including an immense number of Workmen's Compensation cases which, with Malicious Injury Claims, were, at that time, the bread and butter of the Bar.

Despite his appearance, Michael's voice was full of power, reflecting the rocky black hills of his native County Clare, though hardly its wonderful alpine flowers.

There being no criminal trials for that session, the county registrar, Michael O'Dwyer, stood up, bowed and said, 'There are no indictments m'Lord.'

He handed the judge a dingy box. This box was supposed to contain white cloves, a custom from time immemorial. Michael received the gift graciously and Mr Angel, his crier, promptly handed it back.

Legal aid was unknown in those times and, money being scarce, fees were very low. Very often criminal cases were done for practically nothing, though a nominal fee of some sort was expected.

The first case to go on was a District Court appeal. A justice had imposed a sentence of imprisonment on a young girl who was working as a maid in a big house in the neighbourhood of Arklow. Not being able to produce a guinea for counsel, she was represented by a solicitor, Mr Louth of Arklow, a good country practitioner with a sound and varied business.

The girl had stolen her employer's jewellery and some silver spoons. A great case was put up by Mr Louth, explaining how the young lady was under the influence of a man who had falsely promised marriage and that was why she committed the crime, even quoting, much to the judge's interest, from James Joyce's famous short story, 'Two Gallants'. The jewellery had been returned, but apparently the man friend had absconded with the spoons and had not been caught. The girl would not betray him.

'That's a great plea you have made, Mr Louth, great eloquence you have displayed,' said the judge, 'and I'm inclined to be lenient with her. But what about those spoons? The lady will have to get them back, they are valuable spoons, Cork eighteenth century silver. Marvellous craftsmen they were in those days.'

'Yes, m'Lord, I'll do me best if you'll allow me to speak to my client once more again, I'll try her.' He went to the back of the court and had a long whispered conversation with his client.

'Well now, Mr Louth', said Michael.

He came back to his seat and said, 'Ah, this is not the first time I've spoken to her, m'Lord. I'll tell you what, no man could have pressed her more, I've pressed her and I've pressed upside down and inside out and I can't get a spoon out of her.'

Naturally, we all roared with laughter including the judge, and the girl was merely bound to the peace to be of good behaviour.

It was a pleasant start to the day.

Not much interest was provided by the other cases, nor were the barristers' performances particularly sparkling. Gaining later a great reputation for constitutional and criminal cases, MacBride was a very ponderous performer in the Circuit Court where alacrity and ability to shift ones ground is demanded, the judge having to deal with so many cases per day. Vivian de Valera was extremely woolly and Mac Ó Rathaille not less so, except when he worked himself up into a frenzy. He shouted so much at a witness who alleged that his bicycle had been stolen by Mac's client, screaming and shouting at him and turning his back to an imaginary audience in the gallery so that the man didn't know whether his bicycle had a broken spoke in the back wheel or not. Failure to identify the machine, pleaded Mac. Michael Comyn enjoyed every word of it.

The luncheon adjournment was very welcome. Across the road from the chill of the courthouse was an equally arctic hostelry called 'The Wicklow', the word 'Hotel' having been obliterated from its title by command of whatever state body was then busying itself about grading hotels. This one had obviously lost its grade.

The lunch room was at the end of a dark passage at the rear. The room was sparsely furnished, with a large window, with a door presumably leading out to a garden. What I did not then realise was that this chamber was literally built out in the air, designed by some architectural genius who somehow braced it above Wicklow harbour, without any means of support. I rescued Guy ffrench's father from an untimely end one summer's day when he came in complaining of the stuffiness of the court and said he would take a stroll outside. He had the door open when I grabbed him by the arm; it took a glass of brandy to revive him when he looked out the door and saw the cobble stones some thirty feet below. Afterwards he informed a colleague of mine that he would like to send me a brief, presumably in thanksgiving, but he never did.

I asked the young lady what there was for lunch.

'Eggs', she replied.

Thinking of fluffy scrambled eggs, omelettes, or even eggs Florentine, and of the many, many ways they can be cooked, I asked her what way they were done.

'Hard boiled, medium boiled or soft boiled', says she.

And that was the fare. We all sat around one big table. Gus Cullen, the State Solicitor presided, slopped out cups of tea from a huge tin teapot. He was a very able man with a great sense of fun. He had that morning conducted a prosecution against a number of young fellows who were singing and shouting in the street.

'They're all blackguards, m'Lord,' he said, 'except young Behan. He's a real decent young fellow and comes from a very good family. He was misled by the others.'

He was being ragged as to why amongst all the youths he picked out this particular fellow for favourable mention.

'Ah,' said Gus, 'sure his father is a client of mine with a fine farm of land and I have his will in my safe.'

We waited and waited. Then the girl came in with thick rounds of toast and a pot of marmalade, which we immediately devoured. Eventually, the eggs arrived in a bowl.

'Which are these?' asked Gus.

'These are the hard boiled', said she.

Five minutes later the medium arrived and, strangely enough, the soft boiled eggs last of all. Peter Maguire, who later developed a huge practice in Wicklow, and would have been in 'The Wicklow' more times than any of us, remarked that always the hard boiled eggs arrived before the others and he never could get to the bottom of it.

I repeated the train journey every day for two weeks, the duration of the sessions. No one ever considered that I had any existence, though some were kind enough to talk to me occasionally, particularly some solicitors who outside the court-room would smoke a cigarette commencing their conversation with:

'Now, I've a funny ould case in the office, now what would you make of this? I never had the situation before, what would you think of it?' I would be then asked some query, which even the then learned Chief Justice, Tim Sullivan, could scarcely answer.

Putting on a knowing look, I would always reply:

'You'll have to get to the basics, find what the real contract is', or some such rubbish, and I would produce some sort of garbage to ease their problem.

A year later, they began to remember my name.

2

Entering the Four Courts and passing through the lobby, one cannot but be impressed by the marvellous rotunda beneath a magnificent dome. This section of the building is called the Round Hall. Four imposing chambers have their entrances here as in good Georgian architecture. The length, breadth and height of the rooms bear certain recognised architectural proportions to each other, giving them their graceful appearances. The ceilings have been well restored.

The building is not, however, called after these four court-rooms as one might suppose, but after the old divisions of the Courts of Chancery, Exchequer, Common Pleas and King's Bench. If a barrister is said to be 'in the Round Hall', that means he specialises in personal injury, defamation actions or similar common law suits which are usually tried in these chambers. Nowadays, Round Hall people are supposed to have very high incomes, sometimes receiving several thousand pounds for a brief. In the 1940s, however, the recognised senior fee for a common law action with a jury was twelve guineas, or at the very most, fifteen.

The building was stupidly and unnecessarily almost destroyed in the Civil War in 1922. The old library was never restored; its fine furniture and wonderful books were lost, as indeed were most of the public records in an adjoining building. Since our country got its freedom, architectural stagnation had set in and no building of any merit had been constructed. Bounding the courtyard, the Land Registry is housed in a structure resembling a public lavatory. The rebuilding of the Law Library at the rear of the Four Courts was designed by somebody whose speciality must have been hay sheds. This is a chamber without any beauty and without the excuse of being even functional.

Working there for forty-five years I had an air space of about nineteen cubic feet. I sat at a desk about three foot long and eighteen inches in breadth, with a shelf twelve inches immediately above it. Originally, the object of the shelf was to enable books, for which the reader had no further use, to be placed for the Library attendants to carry away. In later years, these men were so harassed and overworked that they could never perform that function, save at the end of the day.

It was, and is, a forum of great animation, a hive of activity, of legal, political, literary and humorous conversation. Three Taoisigh practised as barristers: John Costello one of the ablest practitioners I have known; Jack Lynch who enjoyed an extensive junior practice, particularly in his native Cork; and Liam Cosgrave who would have been a good lawyer had he not been more interested in politics. Charles Haughey and Garret FitzGerald were both called to the Bar but, as far as I know, never became members of the Library. Tánaistí and Ministers and Parliamentary Secretaries abounded, falling over themselves in the Library with joy when their party came into power, and trooping back when they were kicked out. Their political friends seldom let them down and they usually ran into good business.

In the early days before the walls were decorated with large red printed prohibitions against smoking, the predominant smell in the Library was of tobacco, of cigars used by those attempting to give up smoking, of pipe tobacco, and of brands of cigarettes which gave several of the members lung cancer. I regularly brought my robes home to give them an airing outside to try and rid them of the smell before sending them to the cleaners.

The aspiring barrister before he took his call usually purchased a wig and gown. In charge of the senior dressing room was a man whose name was Geraghty. His job was to measure the paraphernalia of the profession. He had a very alcoholic face, spectacles which must have been fitted with incorrect lenses and especially, a very shaky hand. Consequently, it was impossible to obtain a wig of proper fit. As he passed the tape around the victim's skull and wrote the measurements down, the great tremor in his hand was obvious. Collecting my wig from him, in a shiny black box with my name engraved on it followed by the word Esquire and Barrister at Law in bold gold letters, I found inside a horse hair object suitable for the head of a midget. It perched on top of my head, and remained perched there for many years. The wig of one of my colleagues came down over his ears making him look like Dr Samuel Johnson. Nothing could, however, be done about it. Geraghty was in the impregnable position of security and, if criticised, would probably have said that your head had either shrunk or swollen.

In the 1940s the whole administration lay upon the shoulders of Mr Fred Price, a tall man in a dark grey suit, whose office was a roll top desk in the right hand corner of the Library. He bought the Law Reports, collected subscriptions, banked the money, paid the wages and knew the situation of every textbook in the Library. He had no secretary, no typewriter, he did everything by hand, and the place was superbly run. By custom, subscriptions were always a year in arrears and, every November, Mr Price used to go around collecting fees due for the previous years, mentioning also, of course, that the current payment was due 'if you'd like to pay it.' The place is now run by administrators, directors, accountants, chartered or otherwise, secretaries and all sorts of Bob's your uncles, and I don't believe it is more efficient.

There are two large alcoves in the Library, the one on the right is known as the Irish Bay because of the presence of the Irish Law Reports; the other formerly was known as the Smokers' Room where, supposedly, smoking should only take place in a tiny adjoining chamber. There was in the corner, which corresponded to the position of Mr Fred Price's desk, a cupboard known as 'The Shop'. It sold notepaper, stamps, rubber bands, Forms of Civil Bill, Plenary Summonses, red tape and drafting paper. A potential purchaser went to the cupboard and yelled 'Shop', Paddy, the man in charge of that emporium, would come grumbling from his station, where he served as a book 'boy', although he was then about fifty years of age. Unlocking the shop, he handed the purchaser his goods, always saying that Henry Moloney and the bloody shop had him driven effin' mad.

Henry was a K.C. — meaning that he had taken silk before 1922. He had the reputation of being an astute business man on the basis that he had performed a brilliant commercial coup by winding up the Dublin Whiskey Distillers some years previously, and had made a profit for himself. Liquidations and winding up companies at that time were as rare as a rainless February, so Henry, who I think had managed to become chairman of the company, was thus reckoned to be clever enough to accept an appointment by the Bar Council to supervise the shop. He was determined that it made a profit, after all there were a hundred customers and no overheads. There never being any petty cash in the shop, Paddy couldn't give change. Not taking any money for the purchase, he would say, 'You'll see me tomorrow, sir', and consequently, there were many uncollected and forgotten outstanding debts. Henry would accept no excuse and required Paddy, who was a very muddled kind of man generally, to keep a cash-book.

'How can I make a profit selling effin' stamps and rubber bands?' he growled.

Eventually Paddy refused to open the shop, and went missing every time the roar of a customer vibrated through the Library.

Sam was the man in charge of the junior dressing room attached to the Law Library.

'There are no characters left here now', he said to me one morning. 'You should have seen Father Denning.'

Father Denning was neither a priest nor was he any relative of Lord Denning, the famous English Appeal Judge. He, for many years, was the longest practising and oldest barrister in Ireland, and consequently was the father of the Bar. Sam, of course, didn't realise that he was a character himself, but the Law Library was full of people with outstanding personalities and with the correct modicum of eccentricity, combining a strong capacity for humorous observation.

The Law Library is a uniquely Irish institution. A vast office or chamber for barristers, it can be compared to the great Insurance Room at Lloyd's in London. A bell was often rung, not for success of a lost cause, but to announce something like a meeting of the Bar. The original library was a chamber of great beauty, housed upstairs in the Four Courts with two enormous fireplaces at either end. Bays with writing tables, each lined with books, ran the length of the chamber. It was refurbished in the 1880s and, I am sure, in such a manner as to be worthy of the beautiful Georgian complex which comprises the Four Courts. Few Irish people visit the courts, which is a pity. When the tourist trade was good, there used to be as many touring Americans in the building as people with legal business.

The most important job for the Library staff was the 'Door'. A man called Campion held that position in my time. He sat on a high desk at the entrance, preventing anyone from entering the chamber beyond the threshold of which was an imaginary line six feet inwards. He was also required to bellow out names of barristers when asked for by solicitors, and, lastly, to take note of the whereabouts of each member.

To perform the last function, he had a large sheet of paper upon which was printed in alphabetical order, the name of every practitioner. A fresh sheet was used each day. Having called the name requested by the solicitor and receiving no answer, he looked at his sheet and shouted,

'Two, six or the Soup', meaning that he who was sought could be found in either Court 2 or 6 or in the Supreme Court. If in the Library, counsel would trundle up to the door with an anxious or eager or friendly look upon his face, depending upon the caller. Sometimes a man who did not have his work ready for the attorney would hide behind a pillar, dodging the caller. If Campion called 'Coffee' it meant try the restaurant. In later years, when Mr Tom Whelan was on the door, he often said 'I think he is in 11a', meaning the bar. Stentor, the famous Roman general who possessed a voice that each member of the army could hear, would have been only an understudy to Campion, who could be heard in the washrooms a considerable distance away. People learned, however, to hear nothing but their own names when called, which was quite surprising considering the amount of noise in the place. The word 'library' suggests a room hushed and scholarly, but that in the Four Courts was like the Tower of Babel. Campion would vary his call as if he were an exotic bird: 'KINGS' (bellow), 'MILL' (rising to a crescendo) was his method of paging the former Supreme Court Judge; 'HEN'ERY' (bellow), 'MALONEY' (whisper); 'ARTHUR NEWETT' (roar all the time).

Young barristers, including myself, feared Campion. Some detested him because of a malicious, unjustified rumour that, unless you tipped him handsomely, should a solicitor ask for you, he would look down at the sheet and say, 'nothing for him, he never gives me nothing, he's probably not here', or 'I can get you someone else, a good young fellow if you want one.' And the brief would be lost. This story was a fabrication, Campion operated on an unwritten law as far as he was concerned. He received a gratuity of one pound in November when each new barrister was called. At Christmas, another pound was proffered as the tip. Campion always refused it saying, 'No, you saw me when you came in a month ago, thank you indeed, sir, I remember well you saw me when you came in.' But it was obligatory to make the offer.

The 'book boys' comprise the other members of the staff. They were all called by their Christian names. Knowing quite a deal of law, they could find you precedents, that is reported cases, on practically any topic. They knew the year of each Act, they could turn up important sections, and knew the names of the best textbooks for each aspect of law. Joe, Sam, Fred and Tommy were all the truest of Dubliners. The provincials only came when we got the high class secretariat. No additional 'boys' have been appointed over the years, only substitutes, although the management staff multiplied and prospered.

On Campion's retirement, Joe got the door. He had a deep rich, slow Dublin voice. I was shocked in my early days when barristers shouted to this sedate, dignified, elderly man to fetch them a book.

Poor Joe did not survive long, and in his last days there was a great struggle to get him to return to the Church, from which he had many years before lapsed, on account of a problem over a young lady.

Paddy, his successor, having given up muddling in the shop, proceeded to demonstrate that seniority is not the best qualification for promotion. The door confused him just as much as the stamps and rubber bands. At times the situation there was pandemonium, especially on Motion days, which then used to be Fridays. A battle would take place between barristers, pushing their way out, and solicitors, forcing their way in. Each member of the Bar going out shouted 4, 7 or 8 to indicate the court they were proceeding to. Simultaneously, Paddy was expected to write down, as Campion did, those numbers on the sheet. Paddy could never get this right and, to make himself busy, would shout names at random, particularly that of his old pal, Henry Moloney, or would yell to people, 'Ah give me a chance, will ya.' Eventually things got him down so much he started to shout: 'Leave me effin' alone', and at times abandoned the door in mid-stream, leaving it to be taken over by one of the younger boys. Eventually he retired with his 'nerves'. He was succeeded by Mr Tommy Whelan, who held the job with great aplomb for many years.

In appearance, Fred, Sam and Paddy never changed. They

retained their boyish figures and demeanour all through the years. In his old age, Fred fell in love with a lady typist in the Land Registry. He used to stare out the windows hoping to glimpse her. Fred's unrequited love was a subject of mocking amongst the others. He was the gentlest of souls and, on retirement, had a marvellous send-off from the Bar.

The most famous barrister in Ireland when I was called, a man of great presence and fluency with a dynamic brain, was Cecil Lavery, who afterwards went to the Supreme Court where he suffered several years of complete and absolute frustration. The classic briefless barrister was Willie Mason, a small red-haired man, about thirty years of age, who, in the beginning, had a few briefs, by way of compliment from his father's friends, and later did nothing but stand in the Smoking Room all day with his hands in his pockets.

Cecil's seat was in the Irish Bay, quite close to the door. His desk was heaped with briefs, books and papers of all sorts. Coming in from court one afternoon, he set about preparing his cases for the following day. Lost in his study, he heard a rustling sound, and looked up to see Willie Mason.

'Hello Cecil', said Willie. 'Are you busy?'

Suppressing a sigh, Lavery folded his brief, put away his papers, made a space on his desk and said patiently, 'No, Willie, I'm not busy.'

Willie replied, 'Neither am I, Cecil.'

Stranger than the system of calling at the door was the unique telephone system. I'm still paranoid about using that instrument. Calls were made at three coin boxes in a small room outside the Library. A boy of about sixteen years was in charge. Usually he got promoted to the Library, if he could survive. On answering the phone he had to go to the door and have the recipient's name shouted by Campion. This led to appalling delays. Meantime, some other solicitor would be frantically dialling away at the Law Library number. Queues of barristers waited for the phones, one of which was always over-jammed with coins, and occasionally none of them was working.

A new telephone boy arrived shortly after my entry. In idle hours caused by coin jamming and by his deliberately leaving the receivers off the hook, he was seen to be assiduously writing.

Studying to get on in his life? Ambitious with noble Victorian virtues inspired by Samuel Smiles' *Self-Help*? With touching interest, Henry Moloney examined the boy's notebooks to discover, not scholarship, but the nucleus of a fairly hard pornographic novel. The boy, without any chance to justify his status as a potential Henry Miller, was sacked the next day.

The active subscribers and members of the Law Library consisted of about twenty-five Senior Counsel, about sixty juniors and about fifteen others, who had retired from some other occupation, having been called in their early youth. They used the Library as a sort of club, and sometimes did a little work. Now, with the subscription being about twenty times what it was, these types have disappeared and, to my mind, are a great loss. They were ready to converse and impart their erudition to briefless people like myself. Mutual help in difficulty was a great tradition in the Law Library. No matter how large your practice, how many cases you had actively going, you were expected, by an unwritten law, to help and explain difficulties to the most inexperienced practitioner.

As the air in the Library became more foul, the day's work came to an end. Briefs and papers were put into black cloth bags and tied with red silk rope. At five o'clock the 'legal express' arrived. A horse with a canvas-covered cart, managed by a husband and wife, named O'Connor, stopped at the nearest doorway. They collected all the bags, dumped them into the cart and drove around the inner suburbs of Dublin delivering the brief bags. They finished the round at about seven o'clock, and early next morning they collected the bags and brought them back placing them on each subscriber's desk in the Library. This system still continues, except that now it's done by a man or two men with motor cars. The legal diary is brought to each household, and healthy people can walk to the courts without the necessity of carrying papers.

I became a devil to a middle-aged practitioner. I read his briefs, made notes for him, did motions in court when he could not attend. He worked mainly for banks raising mortgages and selling farmers out — work which had little appeal for me. I learnt to speak up and read affidavits so that they could be heard by the judge, but no one ever appeared to fight the financiers.

A solicitor came down one day with a brief tied by red tape and, attached thereto, a cheque for two guineas, my first contested case, to appear in the District Court for a bespoke tailor who was suing his customer for eight guineas, the cost of a suit which, the defendant claimed, did not fit, and counter claimed for two pounds fifty, the price of the cloth he had supplied to the tailor.

The District Justice was Matt Hannon, a man of some scholarship and of infinite piety. Before he made a decision, he would fold his hands and bend his head, and was seen to pray silently for guidance. Usually the Almighty took very little notice. Prayer or no prayer, he could never make up his mind with absolute certainty, so that the most awful villains often got off. He had prayerful doubts about their guilt. He would say,

'Ah, Mister, I have to let you go, because I have a doubt about you, though I have no doubt that my doubt is not the correct one.'

My case excited a great deal of interest amongst my friends who all trooped into the court to listen. I told Matt about the case and put my little tailor into the box. He went down very well. He maintained that nobody could make a proper fit for the defendant, who, in fact, was shaped like a pear. He built up the shoulders for him as best he could, said my tailor. As the newspapers might say, there was a sensational interlude when the defendant retired into the lavatory to try on the suit.

I must confess, it looked deplorable. Firstly, the colour was brown, which no gentleman ever wears. The shoulders sagged, the hips bulged, the trousers were too short. The tailor was asked what he thought about it. He got up and started pulling and chucking at the unfortunate defendant's jacket.

A curious thing happened. I became tongue-tied, overcome with excitement, I suddenly found that my tongue was sticking to the roof of my mouth, my voice was coming in snake-like hissing sounds, I though my jaw was going to lock. Unconsciously, I was reminded of a barrister never known to speak in court and who was christened 'timber tongue'. Matt Hannon, fortunately, was too preoccupied in prayer to notice anything. With his head down and his hands clasped, he meditated for a long time. Suddenly, he said:

'Well I have made up my mind, Misters. I've made up my

mind, I'm deciding for the plaintiff.'

Everyone had enjoyed the battle so much that the parties: customer and bespoke tailor, myself, solicitors and opposing barrister adjourned to the Four Courts Hotel.

Nevertheless, I saw that this was the type of case I would be doomed to conduct if I stayed in Dublin, and I decided to move out on Circuit.

3

I decided to try the unfashionable Eastern Circuit. Because it was near Dublin, its denigrators said that it was full of trespassers who came in for a day and were not real Circuiteers. Many of the towns were close to Dublin and, with proper transport, there was no need to spend a week in a hotel. There was therefore no mess, no Circuit wine cellar and no silver. Posh people used to go on the Leinster Circuit, embracing Tipperary, Kilkenny, Carlow and Waterford at that time. You had to apply to join that Circuit, and for a year the aspiring applicant was called a probationer. Once he had dined a certain number of times, in two or three towns, he was then elected. A strict code was observed. Attendance at dinner was compulsory and punctual. Absence without cause merited a fine 'usually presentation of wine for the cellar'. There was nothing like this in the eastern counties of Dundalk, Meath, Kildare, Wexford, Wicklow.

The turf becoming wetter and wood scarcer, the train became a most unreliable method of transport. Steam could not be got up and the engine would stop for sometimes four or five hours. People practising in Wexford commenced using the bus, which departed from the quays in Dublin and did not stop until it came to Bray.

A journey of 70 miles or so took about five hours. Haltings took place at many public houses on the way, organised, I suspect, by the proprietors bribing the bus crew. Each hostelry was bleaker and filthier than the other. The longest stop was a public house which was built where the waters of the Vale of Avoca meet. There we stayed for half an hour, a few miles on we stopped in Avoca, then Gorey, Enniscorthy, Edermine and finally Wexford. In that time, White's was the Bar hotel. Jimmy, the porter, came to the bus terminus, collected the suitcases and brief bags in a handcart, greeting us all and thanking us all very much, presumably in anticipation. There's a fairly modern song in which every line has many 'thank you very much'es, it could have been composed for Jimmy.

There had been little change in the hotel since the eighteenth century. Great fires welcomed the guests, particularly in the hallway, even in spring and early summer. Fuel shortages didn't seem to affect Eugene McCarthy, the proprietor, who was always there with hearty handshake, as if the guests were all his oldest personal friends. He was extremely warm and kind to me on my first visit. The tariff there was about £10 per week.

The day started with a breakfast of porridge and cream, fish and a dish of bacon and eggs. Willie, the waiter, who was there all his long life, had a soothing voice which would induce a peptic ulcer to accept a mixed grill: 'a little more cream, sir', 'a few more rashers', 'try the homemade marmalade', he would whisper in your ear. There was a large table, unfortunately in the draughtiest part of the room near the window, where dinner was taken and specially cooked for the Bar, most of the other guests settling for tea and an enormous grill. No garlicky nouvelle cuisine chef from a cookery school would have lasted a day in White's. We dined on homemade soup, sole, roasts and plenty of apple pie.

My first journey to Wexford was not by bus. Johnny Esmond gave me a lift in his car. As a T.D. he had a petrol allowance and drove an old Ford car.

It was a bleak February along the quayside in Wexford. The other leading barrister, after Johnny, was Fergus O'Connor, who had gone that day to the local nursing home. A case about trespass and right-of-way was specially fixed for two o'clock in the afternoon. It was one of Fergus' cases and there was now no one to do it, that is, no one oppose the plaintiff for whom Johnny appeared. There was talk of an adjournment, but Johnny spoke up for me, and I got the case. Three hours later I had won it. My client, his brothers, his sisters and his aunt thanked and congratulated me.

'Your first case, before that old judge too.'

My career was made, I considered, as the instructing solicitor was a senior partner in an old established firm which had a very good business. They must give me more work. Looking back on it I don't think I ever did a case with more skill. Not a single brief, however, did I ever receive from that attorney. For many years he hardly acknowledged my existence.

Michael Comyn was very fond of Johnny whom he always addressed as Captain Esmond, in view of a distinguished record in the First World War. When his older brother died, Johnny became a baronet succeeding to an old title. Michael then called him Captain Sir John. We became very good friends for many years and, on his taking silk a short time afterwards, he handed me many cases in which he had been engaged as a junior, and I was able to have him as a leader in cases of mine which required a Silk. There is no greater trial in life than to be a young barrister, with youthful brains and energy, eager to work, but obliged to wait around in the back seats of a courtroom, listening to performances of little skill and waiting for solicitors to come up with a brief.

To attend the Easter sessions, I travelled by the public house bus. On the journey I met an ebullient man, a little overweight, with a fine head of black hair and a moustache. Quickly, he introduced himself to me as Tadhg Forbes, a well known name at the Bar, not because he was doing any great trade at that time, but because of his personality. He was the life and soul of every party. During the long vacation, being a keen Irish scholar and beautiful speaker, he went to a hotel in the west of Ireland where he organised treasure hunts, dances, quizzes, tennis, golf and ping pong competitions.

Having had the usual welcome in White's, and a splendid dinner, sleep became a problem. Jimmy noisily collected all the shoes from outside the doors at any time of the night the spirit moved. He trundled them down to the end of the passage where he banged and thumped with his brushes throughout the still hours of the night. Finishing his task, he tramped down the corridor, thumped the shoes outside each bedroom to make sure that if he hadn't already wakened the occupant, he would do so then. Shoes left outside hotel bedrooms nowadays, apart from running the risk of being stolen, would certainly not be cleaned.

On the Northern Circuit where there was no less a hard drinking lot than any other, the 'Father' of the Bar was an elderly man called Equity Smith. This was to distinguish himself from another barrister, of the same name, who practised mainly in common law. Like Michael Comyn, he was an elderly man with a large stomach. He had a fine white moustache, and always wore a wing collar. Once, after a very good Circuit dinner, Equity having no further work in the sessions, his colleagues brought him to the station to catch the cattle train to Dublin. This was known as the cattle express and had a few carriages for passengers. He was pushed and helped into the compartment, no mean task because of his weight! They chanted goodbye and closed the door. The whistle went, the engine gave a series of indignant snorts and the train began to move. At the same moment the carriage door opened and Equity deposited his boots on the platform. The train went off.

After the usual porridge, bacon and eggs and all, I went down to court to sit in the back and listen. Tadhg was the Wexford State Prosecutor. A criminal case was called — The People v. Connick.

'Bring up Patrick Connick', Michael O'Dwyer, the registrar shouted, and, from the cells below, up the stairs, into the dock, came a man of seventy-two. He stood there facing the judge, who glared at him balefully. He had a bright pink complexion, merry eyes and a massive crop of white hair. A farm labourer, he lived with his employers, earning about a pound a week with his 'diet'. He could not afford counsel and was defended by that very famous solicitor, Fintan O'Connor. He pleaded 'Not guilty'. I could see that Michael Comyn disliked him.

A great voice trembling with emotion, Tadhg opened the case: 'In the year of Our Lord 1935 our legislature in its great wisdom passed a statute for the protection of the chastity of young girls. This is a case in which, when you have heard the evidence, you will truly appreciate the necessity for that great Act of Parliament. The women of Ireland must be protected from men like the villain I am going to describe to you.'

Whereupon Michael Comyn interrupted, 'Does this pontificating mean that this is a sexual case?'

'It does, m'Lord.'

'Then clear the court.'

This procedure of course was entirely unconstitutional, for justice must be seen to be done, however it may effect the feelings of the prosecutrix. Although as a practitioner I was entitled to stay, embarrassment made me leave.   PRUDE!

At lunch time I met Mr Angel, Michael Comyn's usher, a more dignified figure than the judge himself. They were often mistaken one for the other. He told me that he had never heard the like of the roaring and shouting that was going on in court between the judge and Mr Fintan O'Connor.

"Twould split your ears,' he said, 'and they're still at it. The judge is determined to get this man convicted.'

Mr Angel was fond of liquid refreshment occasionally and, at that time particularly, was not in the judge's good books. A week or so before this occasion, when he was expected to drive the judge, he phoned Michael's residence from a public house, from where, to the maid who answered the telephone, he presented Mr Angel's compliments and suggested that the judge might proceed alone to court himself and that he, Mr Angel, would follow at his, Mr Angel's, convenience.

Nobody quite understands quite how important the usher is. He looks after the judge, drives his car, prepares his lunch, makes telephone calls and acts as a sort of secretary. He liaises between the practitioners and the judge. The state of the judge's temper and his health will be conveyed outside the judge's chamber to the practitioners. To succeed in obtaining time for settlement discussions, all is arranged by the usher.

Mr Angel had told me the truth, Michael had gone all out to get the old man convicted and there had been row after row between the judge and the defender. The prisoner was not charged with rape, but an unlawful act of carnal knowledge with a girl under the age of seventeen, which is an offence whether she consents or not. The defence, of course, denied the act, suggested that the girl, becoming pregnant by somebody else, blamed the old man. The case was vigorously contested.

The girl told of her life of housework for the farmer's wife. Her employers had gone to the market with eggs, potatoes and vegetables. Paddy Connick was outside painting the house with lime. When they were well gone he came in and asked for a cup of tea. While she had the bottle of milk in her hand, he grabbed hold of her, knocked her onto a 'forum' — a long bench — and had intercourse with her.

Michael Comyn seemed determined to get a conviction, and nail Connick he did with eighteen months on top of it, a very rough sentence indeed.

That evening in the hotel bar, I was introduced to Fintan by Tadhg, and I joined them. Fintan was fuming.

'Never did I hear such a dishonest and unfair charge.'

Tadhg, no doubt pleased with the result that he had achieved in obtaining a conviction, made sympathetic chuckling noises.

'I don't believe any judge in the country could behave like that old bastard, the dishonest old villain.' He meant the judge, not his client.

'Well I certainly thought he was a bit rough', said Tadhg, licking his fingers.

'I'd like to appeal. A fair court would upset that conviction, without any doubt. I should be into the Court of Criminal Appeal as quick as I can.'

'Why don't you then?' asked Forbes.

'A farm labourer', said Fintan. 'He hasn't a bean. I did his case for nothing and I have, as a solicitor, no right of audience in the Court of Criminal Appeal. I need a barrister, good counsel, and I'm not prepared to finance him out of my own pocket.'

'You can get the transcript if he applies for it himself when he's in Mountjoy.'

'What good's that? I want to show this judge up. I want the Court of Criminal Appeal to be told about him. And unfortunately the transcript won't show his roars and his shouts, his knowing wink to the jury, the sneer in his voice when he dealt with the points which I made, and the way he rolled his old yellow eyes to heaven. That scornful sniff as he shoved snuff up his snout and, of course, that outrageous charge never mentioned any of the points of law favourable to the accused. Incidentally, Tadhg, you didn't back me up much when I made my legal objections to his charge.'

'It wasn't my job. I believe your old ruffian is guilty', said Forbes.

'Ruffian?'

'Well, I didn't mean that', said Tadhg. 'Anyway if you want to appeal, why don't you try this young lad, MacKenzie here?'

Fintan looked at me dubiously. After a while he said, 'Would you do it? There'll be nothing in it for you unless you're extremely lucky.'

I could hardly believe my ears. 'Of course, yes, I'll do it, I'd love to do it.'

'There's a lot of hard work in it,' said Fintan, 'and quite a lot of law.'

I got the brief.

It was a long never ending summer. Transcript of the evidence would not be ready before the end of term, but the court announced that they would sit early in August to hear the case immediately the Note of the Evidence and the judge's charge was available.

As I took the tram into the city on the morning of the case, a

27

fine day in early August, I began to feel my sensation of being tongue-tied. I had been working on the law for the past few weeks. I sat in Junior Counsel's seat in the Supreme Court where the case was to be heard by the Court of Criminal Appeal. I had rows of law reports before me, each carefully marked at the relevant page. As robes are not worn for vacation sittings, I was dolled up in my best suit.

Chief Justice Sullivan was president of the court, a polite man whom I would have regarded as being, like Comyn, 'as old as Methuselah', and whose interest in each case was such that his lips moved as he listened to what advocates were saying, noting everything they said, and repeating every point to himself. Two other judges of the High Court sat with him.

The chamber is imposing, well and tastefully constructed, superior, in my humble view, to the present United States Supreme Court, not to be compared with the beauty of that country's old room now no longer used. The judges must mount a short stairs before reaching the dais. Three ushers come out first, most strangers think they are the judges. One of them carefully switches on a light to illuminate the steps, and carefully and economically switches it off as soon as the court is seated. They stand behind each judge, push in his chair and fiddle around with pens and pencils.

The case was called. My shaking knees just managed to get me to my feet. I started to splutter:

'This appeal, my Lords, is from the conviction and sentence of Patrick Connick, under Section 35 of the Criminal Law Amendment Act. The principal grounds of appeal being that the learned trial judge failed to instruct and warn the jury that it would be dangerous to convict on the evidence and uncorroborated testimony of the prosecutrix.' In other words, the judge should have told the jury it was extremely dangerous to convict on the word of the girl alone. Charges of a sexual nature being so easy to make and so difficult to refute.

Tim Sullivan's jaw moved a few times and he said, 'Very good Mr MacKenzie, very go ˙. We don't need to hear you.'

The message was slow in sinking in, my mouth must have been hanging open. Were they going to throw me out immediately without hearing my carefully prepared argument?

'We've read the note of the evidence, the court thinks it

unnecessary to hear your submission, but we will call upon the prosecution.'

Now he turned to Tadhg. 'What do you say, Mr Forbes? How do you stand over this conviction?'

Tadhg knew that he wouldn't make much of a fist of the case at this stage, but he tried the old argument, that despite the misdirection or lack of direction of the judge, nevertheless there was in fact no miscarriage of justice and the accused was therefore properly convicted and the appeal should not be allowed. The court delivered a short judgment reiterating the point of law to which I have referred.

'The appeal is therefore allowed and the accused is released on bail pending the retrial. Costs of this hearing will be awarded and the costs of a new trial to be heard in the Central Criminal Court in Dublin.'

Outside it dawned upon me that I was going to be paid for my work, and that Connick too would be safe from Michael Comyn. Good old Tim Sullivan, I thought. An old fashioned Irish gentleman, quiet living, dressed in a dark suit, a black hat, a white wing collar, and the shape of an old-fashioned bottle of stout.

Early in November, the case was listed in Green Street Courthouse, an ancient, early Georgian building. On one side of the edifice there is a yard, formerly a place of execution where prisoners were hanged, drawn and quartered. It is now used as a handball alley when the court is not sitting. Unlike any other Irish courthouse, the prosecutors have one robing room, and the defendants another.

Gavin Duffy, President of the High Court, was to try the case. He was a little man with a large beard, the outer half of which was white and the inner, nearest his mouth, burnt brown by chain smoking. Rather than stain his fingers, he held the cigarette secure in a little gold pincers. His experience of criminal law was gained when he acted for Roger Casement as his solicitor. He had a fine melodious voice, a very un-Irish accent, and I could never imagine him drinking a pint, being in a pub, playing a game of golf or fishing, shooting, or anything else of interest to ordinary folk.

Mr Connick greeted Fintan and me cheerfully when we went down to meet him in his cell. I had to explain to him what to say when the indictment was read out to him, in case he did not understand. He was illiterate. He was to shout 'Not Guilty', when asked how did he plead. When informed of his right to challenge jurors, he was not to bother, as Mr O'Connor would look after all that. I explained to him that if he wished, he needn't give evidence, but could rely on the weakness of the plaintiff's case; giving evidence would involve him in cross-examination and one or two mistakes in his answers might lead the jury to disbelieve him. He very readily agreed to this. He didn't think he could stand up to 'them clever fellows'.

Gavin Duffy was a cultivated, polite, careful and attentive judge. He listened even to rubbish and was greatly respected.

Patrick Connick was put up. He came from the cells down-stairs, flanked by warders, and blinked mildly around him. The preliminaries being over, Tadhg got up, opened the case referring to Connick as the prisoner in the dock, and then to the great Criminal Law Amendment Act passed for the protection of holiness, purity and chastity. My client sat in the dock taking a keen interest. Now they have displaced that part of the court and prisoners are allowed to sit behind their counsel, a bad thing, in my view. When the accused are not in a confined space between two warders, they very often abscond when they see things going badly for them.

Like a lawyer's dream, Connick's case went on. The girl sang her evidence out, obviously got by heart. In cross-examination she was contradictory and unsure. She was not believed by the judge, who, I think, was unaccustomed to rustic lovemaking. It was incomprehensible, he thought, that the girl was never kissed, or affectionately embraced. He asked her did he try to kiss her.

'Ah no, not at all', said she. 'The likes of him wouldn't be bothered with that.'

He practically told the jury to acquit the accused.

Fintan and I, while awaiting the verdict, felt extremely optimistic as to the probable result. We didn't, however, reckon on the Dublin jury, who brought back a guilty verdict. But Gavin Duffy reduced the sentence of imprisonment to three months.

I had to face the music and go down and see my client. A number of barristers I know, once the case is over, practically bolt. They can't face the person for whom they have lost a case. Over the years I devised a formula which was invaluable when speaking to a disappointed litigant. I did not say that there was perjury from the other side but: 'That judge was completely wrong. Never did I hear such a monstrous decision from an Irish judge. We will have to think strongly of appealing. We will right a wrong judgment.'

Clients were always mollified by this. Clever counsel (I don't include myself as being one of these) don't lose many cases, firstly because they don't bring bad ones and, if they do, they settle them.

Below, Patrick Connick was drinking a glass of brandy which one of the warders had brought for him, and was smoking a cigarette with the compliments of Fintan O'Connor.

I babbled a bit. I said, 'This is terrible, Mr Connick, really terrible. I can't believe that you are convicted.'

'Ah, don't worry, no man could have done more than you did. You did a great job. You really got her mixed up.'

'But you're going to prison.'

'Ah, sure don't be upset. It wasn't bad when I was in there waiting for the appeal. Most interesting, I can tell you, people I met, and the food was decent enough, better than I had in that farmhouse, especially when that young strap was supposed to be cooking.'

'She told such lies, Mr Connick.'

'Ah she did, she told a few boners all right.'

'But by these lies she has you, an innocent man, convicted.'

Connick's rosy cheeks wrinkled as he gave a huge toothless smile.

'Son, who said I was innocent?'

'You're not?'

'Of course not, I done it, but not the way she said. Sure when the boss had gone, we went upstairs to the bedroom, and I'll tell you, young sir, she wasn't much good anyway.'

This is how I learnt why prisoners never want to give evidence.

After John Esmond's taking silk, Fergus O'Connor became the principal practitioner in Wexford. He was an unpleasant little man in every way. So nasty was he that Eugene McCarthy had to fire him out of White's Hotel. Hot water was a scarce commodity during the war and very limited. Fergus took his bath every morning at half past eight. Arriving down with his special towel one morning, he found both bathrooms locked, occupied by other guests. He went back to his room and turned on the hot water tap in the basin. Having dressed, he went down to the dining-room, breakfasted, took his papers and went to c ⸱t. By that time th₍ re was no hot water left in the hotel.

This was the man to become the terror of the claimants in the Workmen's Compensation actions. He was an unbelievable snob. He referred to women who worked at domestic work as being 'in service'. He never used the word 'Mister' to the workman applicants.

'Now, Mulligan,' he would say, 'tell the judge when you last attempted to do any work.'

'No, that's not good enough, Mulligan. Haven't you a garden around your County Council cottage? Did you attempt to put your potatoes in this year?'

'No you didn't, Mulligan, and that means that you're not interested to get back to work.'

Or, 'Oh yes you did sow your potatoes, well if you can do that, why don't you go back to your work, making blocks for Mr Keogh, your employer? Show the judge your hands, show the judge your foot and your back as far as you can', and so on.

He became the bosom pal of a representative of an English insurance company, which did most of the business in County Wexford of an agricultural nature. Cowed down by the bullying cross-examinations about hands, feet and potatoes, the workmen usually settled their cases for a pittance. Fergus was doing an enormous business. He was known to go down to the office of M. J. O'Connor & Co. where his cousin, Fintan, practised, call to the managing clerk and tell him, 'Dictate a letter to the Commercial Union insurance companies'. He would then walk up and down, after cadging a cigarette and say:

'Now take this down carefully:

'We are glad to announce today the success of the above two Workmen's Compensation cases. Our good fortune was to engage the services of our regular senior junior, Mr Fergus O'Connor, his skill and ability has achieved the result which will no doubt be discussed in your boardroom as the breakthrough in combating these insidious and dishonest claims by compensation hungry labourers.

'In the circumstances and in order to ensure that we still have the use of his talents in future cases, instead of the usual fee of five guineas on the brief, we propose, subject of course to your agreement, to remunerate Mr O'Connor by paying him a sum of seven guineas.

'Assuring you at all times of our best attention.'

Being excluded from the bar at White's Hotel, he and the Claims man proceeded to the 'Pen and Pencil Shop'. In the windows, Waterman fountain pens were displayed, bottles of ink, inkwells suitable for wedding presents, and cherrywood pipes. At the end of the small shop, the counter being on the right, was a heavy brown curtain. Pulled aside, this revealed a bar and there Fergus and his friend toasted themselves for an hour or so before dinner.

Later, when he had apologised to Eugene and had been allowed return to White's, he used to bore us each evening with an account of his triumphs.

'Seven or eight cases disposed of today and all, save that one case you had, MacKenzie, triumphs for the insurance company.'

One evening he unexpectedly said of the claimsman, 'A really nice fellow, Leslie. An awfully nice man, very reliable and very good at his business, but unfortunately not really a gentleman.'

We looked at him in astonishment and Noel Peart said, 'And three times the cock crew.'

4

In 1943, for the princely sum of three guineas plus my bus fare, a further fifteen shillings, I was given a brief to go to Dunlavin, an attractive Georgian village in West Wicklow. The local big shot whom I was to defend was the extensive merchant in the town, and the owner of several farms. He had cured one of his own pigs during Punchestown week to give hams to his friends for racecourse picnics. This great crime was committed during what was then known as 'The Emergency', when, despite the fact that the country should have been bulging with food, it was illegal for a man to kill his own pig and turn it into bacon, particularly if he were to sell it.

I was met at a corner of the main Baltinglass road by a hired car, and conveyed up to the courthouse. There I identified myself to my decent client and went in to do battle with the authorities.

Naturally the posh Dublin solicitor who was paying me this magnificent fee had not travelled down himself. So, when my case was called and I stood up to announce that I was defending my client, the justice, a man called Price, said he would not hear me if I was not attended by a solicitor. I was nonplussed by this and didn't know whether I should ask for an adjournment or hand the matter over to one of the practitioners there who were all solicitors anyway, in which case my lovely three guineas would be gone from my pocket. One middle-aged man who was beside me said, 'Look, I'll stand in for your solicitor. Who is he by the way?'

I mentioned his name.

'Well, I'll tell you, I'd do a favour for any man in Dublin, but there is one bastard I won't do it for and that's your solicitor. He's done me down many a time.'

I was sitting there wondering should I go home when a young man about my own time of life said to me, 'Look here, I'll stand in as your solicitor.'

I was then glad to announce to Price that I could proceed. This justice was an extraordinary man. He was an Irish-speaking, Republican Protestant, who was quite capable of sending my client to jail. Men who chased hares and rabbits or shot pheasants over the lands of the ascendancy were scarified by him. He was managed by his clerk, a ruffian of a fellow, who would whisper to him, during the course of each case. Price was fool enough to listen to him. He was an unattractive sour sort of man, who could be distracted enough by discussions on Irish place names to forget sometimes about the poacher or the tickler of fish. I can't remember what he did to my client, he was not imprisoned.

The young man who befriended me was Tadgh Brennan. Finishing his cases about the same time as myself, he suggested that we go down to a public house where he knew the proprietress who could give us something to eat. Pub grub and that sort of thing were entirely unknown. You might get cups of Bovril with a lump of bacon between two slices of bread. The lady, a homely person, with a black dress and a white apron, asked us into her parlour. While in the bar she poured out two great pints of stout, which fortunately wasn't rationed, and a plate of piping hot, delicious Irish stew. Marvellous of a cold day. Tadgh was not long qualified and had set up practice in Athy. After a couple of more pints he asked me would I come and do his cases in that town where he said nobody seemed to be able to manage Dermot Fawsett.

I was afterwards to practise for almost thirty years there, and I enjoyed most of it even with the difficulties I experienced with Dermot Fawsett as judge. I started with two Workmen's Compensation cases where men injured in their employment were entitled to a weekly payment, not exceeding thirty shillings. It was hard to win with Dermot. In my first case, my client said he was unable to work. He'd injured his back. Dermot Fawsett looked at him sceptically. He had to be careful and prepare himself, because the evidence was written down by a shorthand note-taker and appeals in these cases went directly to the Supreme Court.

Sometimes he would say to the workman:

'Show me your hands.'

He would look at them, poke at them and say for the benefit of the note-taker:

'I am looking at this man's hands. They are massive and strong. Turn up your palms. I am now looking at the palms, they are full of welts and "callouses", it is obvious to me that this man has been working extensively, earning money elsewhere and claiming compensation from his employer.'

Of another he might easily say, 'I am looking at this man's hands, they are moist, soft and pudgy, it is quite obvious to me that this man is an idler, who has made no effort whatsoever to get himself rehabilitated for work. He's not even tried. I doubt if he has even tried to sow the potatoes in his own garden. He strikes me as idle and lazy.'

As I remember, my first client had an injured foot. He was asked to take off his boot and show his foot to the judge, for which he was prepared. The judge then said:

'Show me your other foot, my good man.'

Next thing there was a roar from the bench.

'How dare you wash one foot when you come to court? Go down, sir.'

At the luncheon interval, both my cases were settled. I earned fourteen guineas.

The following week Tadgh had some business in Naas, the principal legal town in Kildare, and always a place for good business, the solicitors being splendid and diligent. Like Wicklow, the courthouse in Naas has two wonderfully attractive rooms which are well preserved. I was leaving the building through the very fine hallway, when there was a bang on the courtroom door, and out shot two people as though they were being ejected from a public house. One short little man, middle-aged, and the other a tall, fair, good-looking young fellow.

'Holy God', said the small one. 'I've never had such a roasting.'

'Excuse me', the young man said to me. 'Would you ever go in and do something for us there? I've seen you operating earlier on and I think you could swing this matter for us.'

'Certainly', I said. 'What happened?'

'Well,' said he, 'we have just been thrown out of court on our ears.'

'So I can see, why was that?'

'We were doing a simple application to have money paid out of funds in court on behalf of a person of unsound mind, when this eejit here', he said, pointing to his older companion, 'made a complete balls of it.'

'How did he?'

'Well, he kept on referring to the applicant as "this ould fellow", and Fawsett roared at him. "How dare you refer to your

36

client as this old fellow, go down", and he threw the papers after him.'

In I went with the affidavits. The judge appeared to have calmed down and I renewed the application and it went through. Thinking no more about it, I went home.

Turning up next morning with no business to do, but merely to sit in the back of the court and listen, and hoping to get work, a letter was handed to me which read: 'Would you be kind enough to call over to the office?' It was signed, 'Paul Wilkinson'. This was from the biggest litigation practitioner in the county, and the young man I had referred to, Martin Salmon, was his assistant.

I went over wondering what he wanted. Immediately I was ushered into his office. He shook me by the hand and introduced himself, saying that he would like me to take all the cases that they had this session in Naas. Their regular barrister, Paddy Bourke, with whom I later became great friends, was engaged in a murder case in Dublin and could not come down.

'In any event,' said Paul, 'I believe he will shortly take silk, we would like you to act in our cases.'

That day was the start of my career.

The man who had been thrown out of court for calling his client 'this ould fellow' was Paddy Fanning, the managing clerk of the office, an old style type who looked after practically everything that was to be done in a busy practice, and at the same time enjoyed the confidence of many clients, who often wanted to see him instead of the proprietor. He became a great supporter of mine.

A visit to his office meant a long harangue about some problem, political or economic. His bête noire was the 'Free State' army, a lot of good for nothing idlers, doing nothing for the country, costing the tax payers a fortune.

He gave me a case to advise, an English thoroughbred breeder, who lived in Kildare, on a problem of some complexity.

He was being sued by an employee, whom he had dismissed for Social Welfare stamps which he had neglected to pay, and he intended to defend the case. I wrote an opinion advising him that he had a good answer to the claim. Unfortunately, I had overlooked a recent Act of Parliament which made my client completely liable for what the plaintiff contended.

I went into Fanning in a great state of nervousness, and said to

37

him, 'On that case of Mr Oswald, I've made a terrible mistake; given a wrong opinion in that case.'

'How did you do that?' said he.

'Well, I don't know, but it is wrong.'

'Ah', said he and looked at me for a long time. 'Is that the first mistake you've ever made?'

'The first mistake of that type', I said.

He reached over, took the telephone and dialled a number.

'Hallo, is that you Mr O? How are you? Now I'm ringing you about that little case that you have coming on in the Circuit Court soon. Yes, it'll be on soon. But I was just thinking to myself how undignified it would be for a man like you to appear in that court and over such a relatively small matter of money, that is to a man of your substance. It wouldn't cut a good figure at all.' There was a pause. 'You'd be better off out of court. Well, I'll tell you what, I'll settle it and you won't have to bother about it.'

He put down the phone, rang the solicitor on the other side and it was all settled in five minutes.

He winked at me. 'There you are, are your worries gone?'

Paul Wilkinson was no slouch as an advocate. He performed extremely well in the District Court. About that time he appeared on behalf of a man who was alleged to have stolen a turkey from a very articulate and forceful lady. The age-old problem of identity and the necessity to be cautious acting on such testimony, was equally present in the turkey case as it is in the highest criminal case. Paul wanted to know how the woman could be sure the turkey was hers. He cross-examined her to that effect.

'Ah no bother,' said the lady, 'I knew it well, wasn't it like a child to me?'

'But how do you know for certain this was your own turkey?'

'Sure, didn't I know its feathers, for example, and the bit missing from its tail?'

'A bit missing from its tail? Is that all, every turkey has something like that, hasn't it, feathers and a bit missing from its tail?'

'Well, I can tell you also, Mr Wilkinson; I knew it by its balls.'

With fire Paul leapt in like the great Marshall Hall, the expert at cross-examination.

'Madam,' he shouted, 'ten minutes ago, when the case was opened and you were giving your evidence, didn't you say your

turkey was a hen?'
'I did.'
'How then could you know it by the balls?'
The lady then began to laugh, 'Ah, Mr Wilkinson,' she said, 'aren't you the dirty minded man? What I'm talking about is the roars and screeches he used to let out, that sort of bawls.'

Noel Peart had the largest practice on the Circuit and took silk at an early age. He developed a good trade in Cork. Recently he was appearing in a probate suit where a very dubious will had been executed by a man who was reputed to be so grossly eccentric as not to be of sound mind, memory and understanding, requisites for making a good and valid will. He left his property to a stranger who had cared for him. The disappointed next-of-kin brought an action to challenge the capacity to execute the document on the basis that he had not, in law, a disposing mind.

The elderly testator lived alone, his only companion had been a small farmer, aged seventy-five years at the time of the action, who gave evidence as to the complete clarity, mental capacity and testamentary understanding of the testator. He had also been appointed executor and universal legate.

This meant that unless the testator could be proved to have had his mental faculties about him at the time he made the will, the inheritance would be lost, and the relatives, however remote, would be the beneficiaries.

Noel, for the relations, suggested that the testator had a number of eccentricities. The executor denied them all, swearing that his friend was absolutely sound.

'Is that so?' said Noel. 'But tell me this, wasn't he given to soliloquising?'
'Wha', wha' did you say?'
'Wasn't he given to soliloquising?'
'Wha'?'
'I think', said the presiding judge, 'you will have to explain the meaning of the word to him. I'm quite sure he's never heard of it.'
'Very well, m'Lord.' He turned and faced the witness and, in a loud voice, said:
'Soliloquising, that means talking to himself when he's alone.'
'Yea, I see', said he.

'Well, wasn't he accustomed and didn't he often talk to himself when he was alone?'

'What?'

'Didn't he talk to himself when he was alone?' shouted Noel.

By this time the witness had thought out the answer:

'Ah sure, be japers sir, sure I was never with him when he was alone.'

It is astounding to reflect that in the 1940s, violent crime was virtually unknown. Old ladies were never knocked down and kicked before having their handbags stolen. Muggings, the word had not been invented. Rarely was there a brutal sexual crime. These are the fruit of violent pornographic videos which, the Garda authorities tell me, are now as corruptive as drugs.

5

In the early days of the State a new office was established, that of a
Circuit Court Judge, whose jurisdiction replaced that of the old
County Court, except that he had wider powers. The Circuit Court
was the tribunal where junior barristers practised in the first few
years after their call to the Bar. Now we have a magnificent bench
of both High and Circuit Court Judges, but in the beginning many
of them were little tyrants, bullies and beggars riding their horses
to death.

About our Michael Comyn nothing wrong could be said. He
was on the side of the underdog and oppressed mostly. Judges
have prejudices which they try to suppress. They may not like
somebody who pursues a particular occupation, like a publican or
a bookmaker, even a parking attendant. Michael's were different.
He might dislike a Kerryman for example. And Michael had a
roguish side to him. Up to the early 1930s, appeals from the
Circuit Court were tried from a stenographer's note of the
evidence given in the lower court. Strangely, the case would be
heard by two High Court Judges, who, if they disagreed, then
decided that the Circuit Court judgment must stand. The
transcript of Evidence had to be approved of and signed by the
judge. Michael was not averse, when he adopted the Note, to
making alterations to suit what he regarded as proper ends of
justice.

I believe in one such case Ernest Wood appealed a decision of
Michael against him. As the case had been tried in court by the
judge it was certain to be reversed by the Court of Appeal. There
was nothing to justify the judge's rulings. The transcript, however,
when Ernest studied it, bore very little resemblance to the action
which had been heard by Michael. The evidence which was vital
to Ernest's case was not there, and it omitted all of the judge's
prejudicial comments. The two Appeal judges affirmed the Circuit
Court's decision.

About a month later, Ernest was standing in the lobby of the
courthouse in Naas when Michael passed through the building,
flanked by several members of the Gardaí, and the county
registrar. As always, entering with great ceremony, and lifting his

bowler hat to anyone who bowed to him, he stopped where Ernest stood.

'Good-day to you, Mr Wood', said he.

'Good morning, Judge.'

'Tell me this. I was very interested in that appeal you took against my decision last November. Did that case ever come off? Has it been heard by my learned friends in the High Court?'

'Indeed it has.'

'You don't say. And tell me now, what was the result?'

'Well, Judge, the court upheld your decision.'

'You don't say, you don't say', said Michael. 'Ah well, that's probably right, and of course, Mr Wood, you can't win every case.'

'I thought I'd win this one', said Ernest.

'And what happened?' asked the judge.

'The transcript didn't bear out the evidence I sought to rely on. In fact, the stenographer, by some misfortune, had omitted some very vital and important aspects of the case.'

Michael took off his glasses, polished them and, looking at him with great astonishment, said, 'You don't say, Mr Wood, you don't say. Surely that could have never happened, or if it did how could it have happened?'

He gave a little laugh and walked up to his chamber.

His patience and tolerance of barristers was immense. He never rebuked the dimmest of practitioners. When they floundered along he would say, 'I'll never make barristers of ye', and let them plug away, in complete contrast to the offensive attitudes of some of his colleagues.

A number of cases were put in for the first or second day of the Sessions. Sometimes these are not reached. Criminal trials came first, then Workmen's Compensation, Malicious Damage, Ejectment and Equity cases, and then ordinary Civil Bills, not forgetting the remunerative part of a Circuit Court practice: publican's licensing business. Thus, a wide experience would be gained, even by listening, by a young practitioner. People who do not go on Circuit, never really learn how to conduct cases.

On the first occasion I went to Naas, civil cases were set down for the first day on the basis that a criminal was going to plead guilty. The stubborn fellow, however, when indicted shouted: 'Not guilty', and, instead of an admission by him of a fairly minor crime, his case had to go on. It was likely to take several days.

Not expecting that the court would be occupied by this trial, a solicitor had come over from Portlaoise to move a simple application grounded on an affidavit, expecting to be back in his office before noon. He had a few drinks at lunch on the first day. Afterwards he had some more, and this was followed by a day long session on the second day.

On the third day he was really stupefied. He sat in the well of the court, which in Naas resembles a bear pit below the judge's bench. During a lull in the proceedings he suddenly stood up on his feet and shouted:

'M'Lord!'

Mick Comyn just looked down over his spectacles.

'I move in the matter of the Settled Land Acts and in the matter of the Trustees Acts and in the matter of Moloney infants. I have an affidavit.'

Michael said nothing. The solicitor began to read. He had difficulty in focusing on the words. Eventually, in exasperation, he threw the papers towards the bench and shouted.

'Here, read the effing thing yourself.'

We waited in stunned silence.

Michael said calmly to his county registrar, sitting immediately below him, 'Mr Brown, hand the papers up to me.'

Barry Brown gathered the documents. Michael looked at them.

'Take your Order, Mister,' he said, 'and with three days' costs.'

Barry Brown, a scion of that old and well established firm, Brown and McCann in Naas, probably the oldest country practice in Ireland always wore a morning coat and striped trousers, a bowler hat was his headdress for the Circuit Court and for the High Court on Circuit, a silk top hat. He maintained a fine store of whiskey in the county registrar's room. Any newcomer, either a barrister or a solicitor, of another county, was asked to partake of his hospitality. The room was furnished with his belongings including a collection of antiquarian books.

Experts, and people who knew all, were disliked by the judge. In one equity suit dealing with the construction of a document relating to an agreement for the fencing in of cattle, Captain Sir

LAWFUL OCCASIONS

John sprang up and said that he had obtained an opinion on the meaning of the writing from Mr Arthur Newett, who was an elderly barrister, practising in the Chancery division.

'Mr Newett,' said Michael, 'ah, a great man, a great man, very learned in equity matters and in the construction of Deeds, Leases and Wills, no doubt Charter Parties and Bills of Exchange, a great man learned in the law.'

Art O'Connor, on the other side, rumbled up his tummy and said that his client had an opinion from Mr Tommy Marnum.

'Ah, a great man too,' said Michael, 'an eloquent man and a man who all night pursues legal lengthy documents of complexity. He knows Coke and every passage in Wolstenholme's Conveyancing.' He paused for a long while.

'They know all about the law', said Michael. 'All about Deeds and Trusts, but I tell ye, gentlemen, I know all about cows.'

An expert veterinary surgeon was testifying in a case before Michael which concerned a gynaecological problem in a mare. He went on in a boring patronising fashion at great length. Eventually Michael shouted:

'You're an expert, aren't you?'

'Yes.'

'You know all about animals, don't you?'

'Well, I've studied that a great deal.'

'Well, tell me, you great expert, what's the period of gestation in an elephant?'

There were many cases dealing with men injured in their work, based on a 'no fault system', but, in Workmen's Compensation actions, the claimant had to prove that the accident which injured him took place when he was engaged in doing something arising out of his employment, not on a 'frolic' of his own. The occurrence had to relate to some obligation of his employment.

Many barges used to traverse the Grand Canal, and one particular applicant for compensation said he fell off his bicycle when his employer claimed he should have been on the barge. The man maintained that he was on a message for the boss and he had to get off at the eleventh lock to rejoin the barge at the fourteenth after he had performed his task. The employer denied there was any need for him to have left the craft.

44

'Tell me,' said Michael, 'you know this area well where you were cycling?'

'I do.'

'And tell me,' said Michael 'isn't there a nice public house half way between these locks — all out on its own?'

'There is', said the bargeman.

'And there is an attractive young widow there too?' asked Michael.

The man looked at him. 'Ah yes, there is', he said.

'Did you stop in there?'

'Well, I went in and I had maybe a glass of stout.'

'I see. The widow and a glass of stout.'

Then he looked down on all of us and said, 'Gentlemen, sailors are sailors the whole world over.'

He was also partial to travelling people. He did not condone, however, sexual crimes by the travellers. He once tried a case which was vigorously defended by the accused on the basis that he really did nothing to the young girl who had charged him with molesting her.

When cross-examined about his activities, he eventually admitted that although he had not had intercourse with her, he may have given her a 'flick of the boss'.

Michael relished this and repeated it. The man was found guilty by the jury and Michael asked him to stand up.

'Tim Connors,' said he, 'I'm sentencing you for the offence for which you have been found guilty. Three months for yourself and three months for the boss. You will serve six months in all.'

The workman, as I have said, was compensated on a 'no fault' basis. The maximum he could obtain was an award of thirty shillings a week.

When I got going in practice, I used to do many of these cases for which the fee was three guineas and, as a judge certified that it was necessary to charge two guineas for a consultation, you had to know an immense amount of law and an immense amount of medicine to be successful in this field.

The standard work on the subject was written by Barney Shillman, who also wrote a book on licensing. He was a cheerful little man, very popular in the Law Library. On the publication of his book, the insurance company gave him a considerable number of cases. Having been called to the Bar rather late in life, he had no experience of the conduct of actions and was completely disastrous in court, although he knew everything about the law.

Before Chief Justice Sullivan, he was arguing a point in a case where he was appearing for the injured workman. It was obligatory on the man to give notice of the accident to his employer, and this man had not done so. Barney made the point that that was irrelevant, the employer knew about it anyway. The employer argued that there was no accident at all.

Barney battled away. Tim Sullivan was presiding and, his jaws moving all the time, taking in every word Barney said. Eventually, in exasperation, the Chief Justice interrupted the learned advocate:

'Mr Shillman, this man told nobody about the accident, is that not so?'

'Well, it seems to be the case m'Lord.'

'And not only did he not tell his employer, or any of his friends, but he never even mentioned it to his wife. What would you say to that?'

Barney waved his hands. 'All I can say, Chief Justice Sullivan, is that there are very many things we married men never tell to our wives.'

Tim was not amused.

A young lady was convicted by a District Justice of dangerous driving. He actually ordered her imprisonment. I think this was because somebody was killed in the accident, although the lady driver was very little to blame. It was a monstrous sentence.

Paul Wilkinson defended her and he pleaded that the offence was not very serious as far as the danger was concerned, and that the girl was of great repute and a splendid character and he called her parish priest.

The parish priest spoke of her in glowing terms, saying that she looked after the poor of the parish, she provided the flowers for the church, attended Mass and Communion almost every day, and there was no activity connected with the youth of the parish or the downtrodden of the community, or the sick, that she did not interest herself in and help such people. 'In fact,' he concluded, 'I will tell you m'Lord, she is a living saint.'

'I'll tell you what I'll do', the judge said. 'The prison sentence is gone, but I'll turn this living saint into a walking saint and take away her licence for three months.'

In my first year, mainly as a result of Mr Connick's case, I earned the princely sum of one hundred and forty six guineas. In my second year, although I went religiously to every town, sat in the back of the court day in and day out, I only earned five guineas, and I was beginning to get very tired and fed up with the whole thing. I applied for a job as a war correspondent for Reuters.

I was confident that I had a chance of getting this as I was literary and wrote in a fairly good style. However, the job went to a man who had been called to the Bar shortly after me, had gone into the Irish Army, and had attained the rank of Temporary Captain. Of course for a war correspondent job, on the face of it, he was ideal.

He was to lose it three months later because he refused to go to the front in Burma where all the fighting was taking place.

Eventually the day of Michael Comyn's retirement arrived. He sat in Naas Courthouse for the last time and finished his work on a summer's afternoon.

In the dressing room, we took off our robes rather gloomily. Mr Angel then arrived, knocked at the door and said, 'His Lordship would like to see you all in Mrs Lawlor's Hotel.'

There we assembled in the back room. In came Michael, battered homburg hat, black jacket besmirched with snuff, and a striped trousers. He looked around.

'Well boys,' he trumpeted, 'twelve balls of malt.' And there was no other drink provided. He bought another round which was followed by libations from the well-heeled barristers.

Eventually, there was a choking noise and I looked around to see one of my friends, his back to the wall, sliding down slowly on to the floor and falling on his face.

Michael, with great concern, went over, pulled the boy up, had one look at him and said, 'Poor fellow will have to stay the night.'

The 'poor fellow' afterwards became one of our most distinguished Chief Justices.

6

People are sometimes appointed to be temporary judges in the Circuit Court. A judge or even two judges may be ill and there is an accumulation of cases waiting to be heard. Paddy McHenry, an able little man from County Tipperary, was one such temporary judge. He was expected to succeed Michael Comyn.

You could not call him a very polished performer, but he was a determined one. Invariably he wore the English barristers' outfit: striped trousers, black coat and waistcoat — garments which he seldom cleaned or pressed.

In the early 1940s he fairly prosecuted the IRA, who returned the compliment by chaining him to the railings of the Killiney railway station, and covering him with tar and feathers. Notwithstanding his abominable experience, Paddy announced he would continue to do his duty. His picture appeared in the *Evening Mail*, the feathers still sticking to his black hair and black coat.

As judge he started off extremely well. He was a revelation, polite and painstaking, an example of what a perfect judge should be. He was determined to try cases according to law and according to justice and to hear everybody. It was certain that he would soon be made permanent and assigned the Eastern Circuit.

However, a latent propensity for the bottle took over. As he had previously been a prosecutor against subversives, he had an armed guard to protect him. There could be no more ghastly time in the life of a Circuit Court Judge than the evening, spending it alone in a sitting room. Not being able to suffer this, Paddy made the mistake of drinking in hotel bars.

There was a row one evening in a bar, somebody threatened him, matters became serious and Paddy ordered his guard to draw his gun.

He had to resign. He left the country, having been called to the English Bar, and went to live in Liverpool where he practised very successfully on that circuit.

He was replaced by Dermot Fawsett, formerly a civil servant, who came to the Bar rather late in life and ultimately obtained the job which he wanted from the first day he set a wig on his head.

He was in my view very difficult and the second most unpopular judge I have known.

Temporarily appointed to the Southern Circuit which consisted of remote towns like Listowel, Killarney and Ennis — that is, remote from Dublin — he was to replace Ned McElligot, a roughneck, and as ignorant a man as could be found anywhere. If Mac ever could be said to have a mind, it was viciously directed against barristers he did not like. Ollie Moriarty, a member of the Circuit, who was badly shot up in the First World War and had to wear a steel plate on his head was, on his reappearance out of uniform, told by the judge that he would run him off the Circuit, and he did by every kind of offence and cruelty. Perhaps he felt it unpatriotic for an Irishman to endure the hell of the trenches.

Judge Fawsett arrived to take up his appointment in Listowel to find the judicial chamber locked. He robed in another room. At eleven o'clock sharp he marched out onto the bench. Simultaneously, through the door of the judge's room, emerged Mac who attempted to put Judge Fawsett from his seat. The audience waited for fisticuffs. Pandemonium ensued and the Sessions had to be abandoned.

After Paddy McHenry left his native shores for Liverpool, Judge Fawsett was assigned to the Eastern Circuit. I went down to Wicklow to take my usual place in the back of the court on the day the great man first sat.

The barristers' benches were at right angles to the judge's seat. Criminal business was the order of the day and the court was crowded with jurors, lawyers and witnesses. Just before the judge came on the bench, Tadhg Forbes, who was there to propound once more the virtues of Criminal Law Amendment Acts spoke to me.

'Do me a favour, Pat', he said. 'Go and ring up Goodbody's office in Dublin and give them a message, here write it down while I tell you what it is. First the telephone number.'

I busily started to write and was so absorbed in what I was doing I didn't notice the judge's entrance. The next thing I heard was a staccato Cork accent shouting at me.

'You, you sir, would you not have the courtesy to stand up when the judge comes in to the court?' He had the habit of always referring to himself as 'the judge'.

My face could have ignited a thousand Halloween bonfires as

49

I stood up and stammered my apology.

'Why did you not stand up?' said he. 'Why did you not show respect to the judge? I hope you are not typical of young barristers of today.'

I said my attention had been distracted, that I meant of course absolutely no rudeness, but I was taking down an important message for a colleague.

'No excuse, sir, at your age, you should respect the judge.'

Tadhg then stood up and made the whole thing worse. Seldom have I been so mortified, but I suppose it was my fault.

Some days afterwards, in private, Judge Fawsett said how sorry he was about the incident. His ulcer had been troubling him, a reason which was frequently advanced as an excuse for his impatience. It would have been far better had he said this openly in court.

Life on the Eastern Circuit, from being cheerful and happy-go-lucky, changed into a situation of tension and anxiety. The solicitors were cowed as much as we were. There were no smiling faces outside the courtroom, no laughter or jokes in the Bar room.

From Wicklow he went on to Wexford where there was no criminal business, but a great deal of equity cases. People from the mouth of the Slaney, I have always felt, are different. Michael Comyn used to say that they were Normans. One day when extremely angry with a young man, who was a defendant in a breach of promise of marriage action, and who had seduced the girl, asked all of us in court did we not all see the Norman face on him, with his long aquiline nose and black hair. Then he soundly decreed him in a large sum, not only for his plundering ancestry, but for his faithlessness to the girl.

On Dermot Fawsett's first day in Wexford, there were many applications to the court. In one case an order was sought for the termination of an administration suit, that is a case to discover what the assets of a deceased person are and to distribute them to those entitled. The proceeding was known as a Motion for Further Consideration.

Noel McDonald, then an up and coming junior practitioner, who later became a great friend of mine at the Bar, had the case and proceeded breezily through his application which seemed to be word perfect. The judge scrutinised everything.

'Now, Mr McDonald, there is just one important matter', he said. 'Tell me, how do I know this man is dead?'

'It's not disputed, m'Lord. Those entitled are all relatives.'

'That may well be, Mr McDonald, but as you know the only real proof of death that can be accepted by the judge is the Death Certificate, a certificate of registration of his death.'

'Well, m'Lord, all parties are agreed that he's dead and neither his birth nor his death is registered. This omission occurs frequently in country places.'

'Then, Mr McDonald, I cannot assume that the man is dead.'

'We have been litigating over his property for the last two years,' said Noel, 'and every body knows he's dead.'

'For all I know, you may be litigating about the goods of a man who is still alive and who may walk in here tomorrow. He may confront the judge and demand to know what's wrong and where is his money. Mr McDonald, I am going to dismiss this case, costs against your client.'

'I think I'll prove beyond doubt to the court's satisfaction', said Noel, 'that the deceased is dead.'

'Don't call him the deceased.'

Ignoring him, Noel shouted, 'Come up, Peter Devereux.' A country farmer came into the witness box and took the oath.

'You are Peter Devereux.'

'That's right.'

'Did you ever have a brother called John?'

'Who's John?' said the judge.

'That's the deceased person, m'Lord.'

'So called deceased', said Fawsett.

'Do you remember your brother John's becoming ill?'

'I do, I do. That was on the Tuesday before Ash Wednesday.'

'And was he confined to bed?'

'He was.'

'Do you remember the doctor coming?'

'Ah, indeed I do and it was a very sorry day. He said he had something wrong with his heart and he wouldn't last long. The doctor said to get the priest.'

'And do you remember the priest coming?'

'Yes I do, me wife and meself came over and we set up the candles and we saw him getting the Holy Extreme Unction.'

'And what happened after that?'

51

'Well, he died.'

'Now be careful, Mr McDonald', interposed the bench.

'Tell us what you saw, Mr Devereux.'

'Well, I saw John lying there with his eyes shut, and we were all crying and saying how sorry we were.'

'Do you remember the undertaker coming?'

'I do.'

'Did you see John lifted into the coffin?'

'Yes.'

'And do you remember the lid of the coffin being screwed down?'

'I do, we were all there and that was before he was taken to the church. He was taken to the church that same hour and remained there the whole night.'

'And next day, did you attend the Mass?'

'I did.'

'And did the priest praise him from the altar?'

'He did, he said what a fine man he was.'

'Did you follow his coffin to the churchyard?'

'I did, we all walked behind the hearse.'

'Have you a family plot?'

'Be dad we have.'

'Did you see the coffin lowered into the grave?'

'Aw, I did, I did.'

'Did you see the earth thrown on the coffin?'

'Indeed I did.'

'Did you see the grave filled up?'

'Yes, we waited there till the very end.'

'Now you've told us about the funeral, about the grave being filled up and all the earth on it.'

'I have.'

Noel paused dramatically.

'Now, tell me, have you seen your brother since?'

There was a great laugh, Fawsett got absolutely furious, but he had to concede that the man must be dead, and the relatives got their share.

7

Becoming a barrister involved, in addition to passing examinations, the keeping of twelve terms commons at the King's Inns. An obligation to eat four dinners each term in the dining hall, recorded and presided over, by some of the benchers, was a prerequisite to admission to the degree of Barrister at Law and call to the Bar. One guinea provided six dinners, consisting of a glass of beer, soup, fish, joint, pudding and coffee with half a bottle of wine thrown in. The food was excellent. On a special evening each term there was a full bottle allocated to each student and an extra course. Although my palate could not be said in any way to be refined, I thought the wine terrific. Sitting at tables of six, it was a fair bet that one half of the boys did not drink, and their wine was then demolished by the others. Embarrassing occasions resulted, therefore, when people had to be assisted from the hall, collapses were not unknown.

The elections of new benchers were occasions of celebration, on the newcomers dining at the benchers' table for the first time, resulting in a large attendance of judges, Senior Counsel, barristers and students. A great banquet was provided with good wine for the students and, for the benchers, Grand Crus and champagne flowed.

In the foyer of the Library of the Inns, among other exquisite pieces, is a magnificent porter's chair and a beautiful Irish made Georgian settee. The chair used to be occupied by a very rotund, ex-naval rating, called O'Keeffe, in whose hands rested the safety of the entrance.

Picture a pumpkin set on top of a barrel of Guinness, that was O'Keeffe. His use of the English language was to be expected, not of a seaman who had been in the Battle of Jutland, but of a jack tar forced into the service of the navy, by a press gang in the eighteenth century. Like some modern writers, the use of the past tense was unknown to him:

'I goes into the battles and the wars, after that I gets home and fetches this job here. Mr Hewitt Poole, he finds me here a good position, that's where I be now, a happy soft job.'

Waiting at the dinner table during the term was part of his

duties. For this he was required to wear a livery of brown stuff, knee-length braided coat, a coloured waistcoat, trousers that looked like plus fours, made of dung-coloured plush, white stockings and buckled shoes. As the Bar had never come out of mourning for Queen Anne and always wore robes of black, so also was the livery retained in the King's Inns until the embarrassed attendants at dinner refused to wear it any more. O'Keeffe had always to run through a barrage of small boys for the hundred yards or so from the gate of the Library to the entrance door of the Inns, pelted with rubbish, insulted with screeches of laughter and jeers.

As students, my friends Brian Walsh, Paddy Leonard and Gerard Clarke in the summer went to work quite a lot in the Library. When I say work, an odd book was taken out and perused for a while and those who smoked — nearly everyone did at that time — got up and went down to the hall, or if the day was fine, down to the garden where there were seats in the rear. I used to chat with O'Keeffe. He acknowledged himself a lapsed Catholic:

'Somehow and I gets the job here, were I going to Mass I never would. I go to the church sometimes, so that they can see me to be a good Protestant.'

At the middle of September the Library would be crammed with barristers, settling to work as the vacation drew to an end. Jack Costello, former Taoiseach, told me that as a junior, August was always his busiest month, and when I was well established I came to realise that a considerable amount of money could be made in August, by donkey work at the desk. Urgent matters also came up frequently. James Fagan, a prominent Dublin solicitor, during a hot August heatwave, asked me to attend a consultation with Jack in James' palatial Georgian office in Parnell Square. It was furnished in a manner suitable to the period of the building.

Before we met the clients, James impressed on us how important the Managing Director considered himself to be. Though his name was spelt Bullock, it was to be pronounced Bewelook. Jack, never good at names, made very little comment about this, the legal problem was what concerned him, as it always did, so he absorbed himself in the strategy of the case of the law applicable. Through the consultation, he addressed the Saville Row-suited Managing Director, never calling him anything else except Bollock or Bullock. But he did obtain the injunction on the following day.

There is a famous Victorian painting portraying an old sailor from the Spanish Main pointing out to the distance across the harbour as he tells his yarn to two small boys listening to him enthralled, so did I enjoy O'Keeffe's yarns. Towards the end of the vacation, I was sitting in the porter's chair when a man the double of Billy Bunter, mounted the steps and came in. A small fat man with heavy gleaming glasses, large tummy, a black jacket, black waist-coat, watch chain and striped trousers. He had a little moustache. He walked with a cocky, confident air.

'Good day, sir', said O'Keeffe smartly, touching what once might have been a forelock.

'Ha, O'Keeffe, ha, how are yeh today?'

'Well enough, sir, thank you.'

'"Deed yehare, like myself.' He had a very pronounced Dublin accent and he went on upstairs.

'Know who that be, sir?' O'Keeffe asked. 'Mr John Devlin, he 'as a great practice. Great man.'

At the Bar I got to know him very well, but I was warned about him at the beginning. He displayed the utmost friendliness and eagerness to help any new barrister.

'Try and cut your teeth on this little easy thing before the Master, it's the simplest little job before Judge O'Byrne', he would say to some unsuspecting victim and hand him papers. The eager young man would hasten into court to find that the papers that he held in his hand contained a time bomb of the most confounding problems. The young practitioner was usually thrown out by the judge and would come red-faced and stumbling in a dazed condition back to the Library.

'How did you get on? Ah, sure not to worry, you'll get better next time.'

But John really never wanted to hear about the disaster.

At that time, there was a man who had retired from the legal department of the army. His name was Manus Noonan and he subsequently became a District Justice. Whether he had learned anything by the time he had achieved that judicial office is debatable, but he certainly knew nothing as a result of his career in the army. He sat in the Library looking into space. Approaching him one day, John said to him:

'It would be a very good experience for you, Noonan, and something for you to be able to sit behind Cecil Lavery, the best man in the whole of this place, indeed in the whole of the country, north and south and indeed in London and everywhere; to sit behind him for half an hour or so and take a little note of what he's saying and you'd learn how to open an appeal in the Supreme Court.'

'Oh, that would be great, John,' said the other, 'but I hope I wouldn't have to do anything, would I?'

"Deed you wouldn't, 'deed you wouldn't, not at all, not at all. You'd hold the junior brief and take a note for a while, until I've got over a few of me problems here around the Circuit Court, before that awful man, George Shannon and I'd get back to you and off you could go.'

Noonan said he would welcome the experience.

'You'd like the opportunity then?' said John. 'All you have to do as I said is to sit there, sit there comfortably for a while, in case he'd want a book or two brought in to him from the Library, and then I'd be in there and off you'd go. Meantime the Supreme Court Judge would know you're back in practice. They all know that you were working at legal things in the army, but it's not quite the same thing, and I'm sure that they would be very glad to see you, and the solicitors would note you as well.'

'If that's all I have to do,' said Manus, 'fair enough.'

"Deed, that's all,' said John, "deed it is, 's all indeed.'

Manus therefore took the papers saying he'd read them and sit in the junior bench behind the great man, taking notes and fetching books if required.

At ten minutes to eleven the following day, Manus went into the courtroom, the case being listed for the hour of eleven. Manus' solicitor was there, so was the opposing side in full force with all their legal team, but there was no sign of Cecil Lavery. Noonan was unperturbed. He sat down, looking pleased with himself, and started to study the papers. After the first few paragraphs of Devlin's brief had been perused there was a cry of:

'Silence, all stand.'

Out trundled the ushers, each behind the chair of his respective judge. When their Lordships were seated, the Registrar called the case. Nobody spoke, nothing happened. The Chief Justice looked down and saw Manus and said:

'Are you for the appellant in this case?'

'Well,' spluttered Manus, 'yes I am. No, I'm not. I think I'm not. It's somebody else.'

'What do you mean? Are you appearing for the appellant in this case?'

'Well, I hold the brief. I do, I have a brief here all right, but I'm not really in the case.'

'If you're holding the brief, then will you kindly proceed to open your appeal.'

'But I'm only here for a while, I'm only here waiting for Mr Lavery to come. He's to do the case. Would your Lordships adjourn for a few minutes? I don't know what's happened to him.'

'The court is not concerned with Mr Lavery's absence. You're here to represent the appellant, now proceed to open the appeal.'

Manus clutched the papers and started to read. The first document he seized was the Notice of Appeal, which he proceeded to read out verbatim. Most of the judges were amused, but the Chief Justice then was not exactly a man for hearty laughs.

'That is no way to conduct a case in this court', he thundered. 'You don't appear to know anything about what you are doing.'

'But that's quite right. I don't know anything about it. I don't want to do it, I can't. I'm not really conducting the case, I'm merely waiting for Mr Lavery.'

'Once you accept a brief, it is your duty to be ready to conduct the case.'

At this juncture, the door opened and Cecil came in. Manus gasped with relief.

'Ah, here's Mr Lavery', he said.

'We're hearing you and your submissions,' said the Chief Justice, 'continue with your argument or at least begin your argument, for you've said nothing so far. Open the appeal to the court.'

And so the agony went on until eventually Lavery got to his feet, intervening, explaining the situation. He then commenced, in his usual polished fashion, to conduct the case.

With weak knees, almost fainting, Manus staggered out of his seat and made for the door. In the dark recess at the back of the court, a sudden shaft of sunlight touched a pair of glinting spectacles, small beady eyes glared from behind, a look of disgust was on the face of John Devlin, who of course had been present all the time.

As Manus went out, John caught hold of his arm.

'Jasus, Noonan,' he said, 'you made a right hames of that.'

Because he was amusing and had an apt turn of phrase, John was liked by George Shannon, the presiding judge in the Dublin Circuit Court.

Even lay people who watch television know that leading questions which suggest the answer to a witness should not be asked of one's own client. This rule of law John ignored. I heard him conducting a Personal Injuries case for an old lady who was knocked down when crossing the road. It was obvious that she never saw the car that struck her. He proceeded to question her:

'Now, Ma'am, pay attention, listen to me, when you got to the edge of the road, tell us exactly, what did you do?'

'Sir, I went across.'

'Ah yes, but what did you do? What way did you go across?'

'I went across quickly', she said.

"Deed you didn't', said John. "Deed you didn't. What did you do now when you got to the road?'

'I went across.'

'Ah, not at all, Ma'am, 'deed you didn't. Didn't you look to your left, didn't you then look to your right and didn't you then look to your left again and didn't you look to your right again and did you see nothing coming, and didn't you go across the road, and weren't you hit by a car flying at a tremendous speed at you?'

Even the judge had to laugh.

He was excellent at jogging a plaintiff's memory:

'What injuries did you suffer? Were you badly hurt?'

'Ah yes I was, sure I was very bad.'

'What happened to you?'

'Well sir, 'em I can't remember very well.'

Then John would hold up his thumb and point to it.

'Oh yes, oh yes sir, I hurt my finger very badly.'

John would then put his hand on his nose.

'Me nose was broken.'

John would touch his forehead.

'Ah yes, there was a cut over me eye', and so on.

John got a case to defend a young man who was charged, with others, with breaking and entering a factory and stealing whatever was in the premises. In criminal cases, the accused seldom gives evidence, but relies upon the weakness of the prosecution's case, challenging the witness in such a way as to induce the jury to have a reasonable doubt and, therefore, in law being entitled to an acquittal.

John did not call his client, but took a rather unusual course, calling witnesses as to the man's character. He produced a priest who commented on the respectability of the family, the honesty of the parents and his distress at finding John's young client in the terrible situation being charged and sitting in the dock.

At the conclusion of the evidence counsel for the other accused addressed the jury, and John's turn came last. He did so in eloquent and moving terms. His voice pitched up and his words were shouted out with rapidity. His client was a young man of twenty-one years, he said, and for twenty-one years he'd been walking around the city of Dublin, without a stain on his character and, please God, for another twenty-one years he would be doing the same, if not three times twenty-one.

'Still he's a young man of great character and repute and yeh heard his witnesses including his priest.'

Having taken the case to heart, John remained gloomily in the ill-furnished uncomfortably chilly barristers' room in Green Street Courthouse, while the others went across the road to a hostelry, known as the Court of Appeal, no doubt for cups of Bovril and other warming cheer.

Unexpectedly, the jury came back. John received the verdict and went across to the pub. He was greeted with chortles and back slapping and congratulations on his great speech about the twenty-one-year-old man for twenty-one years walking the streets of Dublin, an amazing achievement. What a remarkable baby he must have been.

John took it in good part. 'I'll tell you this', he said. 'Do you know what I'm going to tell you? You've been laughing about my client walking the streets of Dublin for twenty-one years, but I'll tell you this, he's still now walking the streets of Dublin, he's been acquitted, but your clients haven't and you can put that in your pipes and smoke it.'

Counsel are supposed to be present in court when their case is called. If not, a second calling is allowed and the next case then taken up. High Court Judges in those days were extremely annoyed if a practitioner appeared to be devoting his skills to cases in courts other than their own.

On one occasion, John, not appearing when his case had been called twice and the list was almost over, trundled into court gasping and puffing.

'Where were you, Mr Devlin?' the judge, Henry Hanna, asked him in an annoyed tone. 'Why weren't you here when your case was called?'

'Don't ask me that, me Lord, please don't ask me that.'

'Why not Mr Devlin? Why not? Where were you?'

'Ah well, don't ask me now.'

'Ah, Mr Devlin, this won't do.'

'Well, if I told your Lordship where I was, it would only make it worse.'

Hanna had to laugh.

Devlin died rather prematurely, I would think that eating contributed a great deal to his early demise.

He took lunch in the Four Courts Hotel every day — an excellent hostelry, well patronised by hungry cattle dealers from the market in Prussia Street — where he consumed four courses, with two helpings of pudding. Ultimately he grew enormous.

Rivals came and tried to usurp John's business but he, like the babbling brook, went on for ever.

Sean Breathnach, who had been employed in the Dublin Corporation, did the Bar and was called in his thirties. He commenced doing a good business although he was an extremely stuttery kind of performer. He became a rival to John. He told me that he was an expert at getting business.

Another colleague who did a fair practice in Dublin was Brian McQuaid, he was called to the Bar a year before I was. He was very able, but somehow drifted away. He was highly regarded by George Shannon. A most dignified man, portly and looking older than his years, he loved wearing a barrister's outfit. In fact, when his wife produced their first baby in the Hatch Street Nursing Home, he would come in to see her at night, bring his work with him, sit down and do it at a table. The nurses used to come in and watch the spectacle. He was not just sitting there busily writing away, but he was wearing his wig and gown. Thus attired, he solemnly laboured away.

One of the juniors in my time, with a big District and Circuit

Court practice, was Herbert Clancy. Very elegant and a perfect gentleman. Like many fluent operators in court, he had a gross dislike of doing paperwork. Giving opinions and drafting pleadings are more important to solicitors than Clarence Durrow-like performances before a judge. Herbert spent a great deal of his time sitting in the Gresham Hotel's Winter Gardens, drinking coffee with other elegant people, chatting away and greeting friends. Under harassment from solicitors, crying out for their draft Civil Bills, late at night he would leave the Gresham Hotel and go to the nearby GPO where he spent an hour or so knocking off the drudgery of paper work and catching the early post. Occasionally, his briefs were found in that hallowed building.

A very gentle soul, who specialised in a field of litigation known as 'Rent Act' applications, was John Coughlan. He wrote a book on the subject which went to two editions. Being very pious, John used to spend his summer preaching on the beaches of English seaside resorts, at least that's what Sam from the dressing-room told me. Later on John became a District Justice, and during his entire career only imposed two prison sentences.

The insurance companies usually employed Felix Sherry, a small aggressive little man with piercing, but refined North of Ireland accent. All litigants who were not his clients were rogues and villains. He was my opponent in my first Dublin Circuit Workmen's Compensation case. He was instructed by Ivan Howe, a bowler-hatted, old-fashioned type from D & T Fitzgerald (a firm mentioned in *Ulysses*). Felix, politely for once, asked me if I was interested in settling my case which was about to commence in a few minutes time.

My client, a decent little Dublin man who had broken his finger, was perfectly willing to return to work, provided he got a few hundred pounds. Accordingly, I went back to Sherry and Howe, who were with two English insurance men. Why they bothered to come over from London for such a miserable case I could not understand. They bore a most remarkable resemblance to Flanagan and Allen.

'My client is quite willing to settle,' I said, 'but I must just tell you about him.'

Ivan Howe, his face red as a beetroot interrupted me and shouted:

'I'll tell you about your client, yes I will. I'll tell you all about
that bloody ruffian. He's a lazy no good idle fellow who wants
nothing but our insurance company's money and he's not getting
any of it.'

Despite Felix's cross-examination in court, my man did very
well and afterwards, half way through, we settled for twice as
much as I would have originally taken.

Felix's cross-examinations were usually conducted in roars
and shouts. At one motorist, who was in collision with his client,
he bellowed:

'And further, I put it to you, I put it to you that you in your
motor car in fact came out of nowhere.'

Even the lugubrious George Shannon laughed.

Ladies found him attractive and he was very fond of them, and
was extremely polite and charmingly mannered towards the fair
sex.

About that time, I got a case to defend a man who was
accused of keeping a brothel in Gardiner Street. There were a
number of prostitutes in court but, nevertheless, the State was
having great difficulty in proving the case. My client solemnly
maintained that he had nothing but respectable married couples in
the bedroom, pointing out their names and addresses in the
Visitors' Books —Mr & Mrs Mulligan from Mullingar, Mr & Mrs
Smith from Rathvilly, and so on. The State Solicitor called a
middle-aged farmer from Mayo who was on his first visit to
Dublin. He recounted that he'd met a lady in a Café in O'Connell
Street, where he was devouring sausages, fried eggs and chips,
who invited him to go down to the Hotel. Naturally he was very
sheepish about this but, he recounted, she asked him if he was
tired and would he like a rest. They booked a bedroom and got
into bed.

'What happened then?' said the State Solicitor severely.

'Well, we started trickin',' he said.

'Trickin'?'

'Yes, that's right, we were trickin' around.'

'What happened after the trickin'?'

'I got up and put on me clothes.'

'Why did you do that?'

'I began to see that she wasn't exactly a good girl and I felt it

62

better for me to leave.'

Despite the flimsy evidence, the District Justice convicted. I had to give all I had to prevent him from being sent to jail, but a hefty fine was ultimately imposed.

On the way out I was congratulated by the ladies who were laughing and giggling at the whole thing. One and all they said:

'Don't forget, son, give our love to Felix.'

8

It is not surprising that members of the medical profession play an important role in litigation. In most cases where damages are claimed for personal injuries, they can be seen on the plaintiff's side giving forceful evidence of permanent disability resulting from the injury, and then for the defendant, of complete and absolute recovery. Psychiatrists are employed in the Family Courts to a great extent. In Probate and Will suits they crop up usually in discomforting roles. For in that branch of the law, it is extraordinary in contests where wills are challenged on the basis of the testators incapacity, one doctor may find the testator completely sane at one o'clock, and another may find him completely incapable mentally at three.

Formerly, doctors were appointed as consultants to hospitals without any pay. Their income came from the allocation of beds in those establishments for the treatment of private patients. Naturally, anything they could earn from the legal system was a considerable bonus.

As they were obliging and accommodating, solicitors went out of their way to facilitate them, and so did the courts, conveniencing them as much as they could by arranging particular times for their evidence. This still pertains. Doctors used to take a chance like the lawyers: if their patients won, they were paid for treatment and for medical attendance at court; if the plaintiff lost, like the rest of us, doctors had to put up with it.

The most sought after witness for insurance companies, and the doctor most involved in litigation, in my time, was Mr Arthur Chance, Orthopaedic Surgeon attached to Jervis Street and Steven's Hospital. Rushing into court and smelling of ether, he would explain to the judge that he had just come from the operating theatre, and could he have a moment to consult his notes. A most formidable man to cross-examine, because he never answered a direct question — he gave a little lecture as if he were addressing students, and the result was long and ambiguous — he was strikingly handsome with silver hair, silver moustache, immaculate blue pin-striped suit; he consulted his notes with the aid of a monocle. It was reputed that insurance companies paid him great fees during the War to travel to country places for the day. A counsel appearing for the employer in a Workmen's Compensation case might get five guineas, it was said that Dr Chance got a hundred and a car to bring him to the courthouse.

On one occasion he went to Thurles, instructed by an insurance company. The case was a Workmen's Compensation review, meaning that a man having been awarded a weekly sum for compensation, the employer sought to terminate it by reviewing the original order, on the basis that he had either wholly or partially recovered and was fit to do some work again. The compensation should then be terminated or reduced.

Opening the case, the employer's counsel told the judge that Mr Chance had thoroughly examined this man and he was satisfied that he was absolutely and completely recovered and could go back to his job. Taking the oath in his clear voice, dressed in pin stripes, grey spotted tie, gleaming hair, but no ether, Mr Chance, waving his notes, commenced his evidence:

'This man, aged thirty-five, told me that he hurt his back lifting a bale of straw two years ago. He then experienced a sharp pain in his lower lumbar region,' he placed his hand at the small of his back, 'here. He had tried to work several times, but could not because of intense pain. Planting potatoes this spring was far too much for him, even if he took his time.

'I examined him thoroughly, during the course of which he said he was no better — the pain was terrible. He had tried some work planting the potatoes, but after that had to stay in bed for three days and he couldn't move through pain and stiffness.' Mr Chance solemnly put down his notes.

'I remember asking him to bend forward, he winced with pain. Asked to touch his toes, he couldn't get his hands even near his knees. When I palpated his back, he jumped in agony. He asked me to stop it "for Jasus sake". He said he believed he would never get back to work, even light work — it would kill him.

'However, I had asked him to undress for the examination and, although he didn't know it, I observed him closely. To take off his trousers he had to pull his braces from the shoulder, undo his belt, he had to bend down to remove his trousers as he still had his shoes on. His back movements during this were free and perfect.

'I observed him again when I told him to dress. He bent down, picked up his trousers with complete ease, pulled them up, adjusted his braces, using all the muscles of his back during this performance.'

'What was your conclusion then, Mr Chance?'

'In my opinion, this man has completely recovered and at the time I examined him was fully fit for work. No objective reason could be found clinically or radiologically for his pain. There was nothing on the examination to justify his complaints, on undressing and dressing, all movements of his back were full and painless. It is my opinion he had recovered and should have been back at work long ago.'

The employer's barrister beamed and sat down. His solicitor smiled and the insurance company man in the back of the court, busily taking notes, gave a complacent smirk.

Ruefully, the workman's counsel stood up.

'I'm calling his local general practitioner, m'Lord.'

'Very well', said the judge.

There could not have been a greater contrast. Dishevelled suit, untidy hair and greasy tie, and a strong rustic accent.

'What's your opinion of the applicant?'

'I know this man well. He can't work, he's got a bad back, he's a genuine character and an honest man and it's my view he'll never again be fit for full labouring work.'

'What did you find wrong with him?'

'Ah, he must have strained his back with a hay fork, the weight was too much. All his muscles and vertebrae are sore. I know all his family and they're all genuine. Workers to a man and woman. He was a rare fellow until he got this injury and I don't think he'll ever get back again.'

He was cross-examined by the employer's counsel.

'You say he hurt his back, what muscle did he strain?'

'Ah, one of those muscles that's attached to the spine, the lumbar muscle, they're all over the back.'

'Didn't you say on one occasion the last time we were here that he had pain up near his neck?'

'Sure he had, it was all over his back, everywhere.'

'Now, Doctor, you're on your oath, don't you know this man is a malingerer?'

'Faith, he's not, he's genuine and cannot work. He might try a job for an hour or so but then he's had it. 'Twould be the bed for

him for days. He knows all about it, I tell you.'
'Were you here for Mr Chance's evidence?'
'I was.'
'Did you pay attention to it?'
'I did.'
'You know Mr Chance is an expert in back injuries, an ortho-
paedic surgeon as well, you're in general practice.'
'Sure, and I maintain that this is not a bone injury, he's got a
right bad back, as bad as I ever saw and it's his muscles are hurt.'
'It is your sworn testimony he can't work.'
'He cannot work.'
'You heard Mr Chance say,' dramatic pause, 'that he could
undress himself without pain, managing his trousers, both dress-
ing and undressing. Have you any comment to make about that?'
'Yes.'
'Well, what do you say?'
'You won't get any work in this town pulling down and
pulling up your trousers.'
The man's compensation was not cut off and he and his doctor
went happily to the nearest pub.

All jury cases were held in Dublin up to the early sixties, when
they started firstly in Cork, and later on in Galway and other large
provincial towns. In these venues the massive awards given were
responsible for the agitation by the insurance companies which
led to the abolition of the jury system. Whether this works out
well for the general public, litigants and insurers, remains to be
seen. At least eighty per cent of the cases listed used to be settled.
During the War, the entire list of cases for the jury term in
Dublin came to about thirty actions. The judge would sit specially
to fix the date of each action early in the term. People got up,
mumbled about their cases and had them listed as far away as
possible. For the first two weeks there were scarcely any trials. A
judge was allocated two cases. If the judge finished, having
disposed of these actions, he went home. Nowadays, of course, he
would take up other work. There are now at least thirty cases per
day.

Paddy Lindsay did a great trade in Galway and was very plaus-
ible before a jury of his fellow countrymen. One time he appeared

67

for a small farmer who staggered out of a public house on a Christmas Eve about midnight. Before arriving at his home, he fell onto the ground and went fast asleep on the roadway. A car ran over him injuring him, but fortunately not fatally. The case was completely hopeless, as in those days there was no apportionment of liability, and fault by the injured party meant the loss of the case. The driver should have seen this object on the road but this would not necessarily give the plaintiff a right to damages. If the injured man were held guilty of contributory negligence, he had no case. However, Paddy had a good judge who was extremely annoyed with a vehement and uncharitable closing speech from the defendant's counsel, who sanctimoniously condemned drunkenness and asked them to award the injured man nothing.

'It is the custom of the people of Ireland to celebrate Christmas in accordance with the Christian tradition of joy and thanksgiving, particularly thanksgiving', said the judge. 'Gentlemen, it would be indeed, would it not, a very sad day for the country if a poor Irishman could not go home from a public house at midnight to prepare himself for our greatest Christian feast and, feeling tired with the weight of drink, decide to lie down on the road, have a nap and refresh himself for the day ahead, without being half killed by a reckless motorist. Please God, gentlemen, things in this country will not change that much.'

There was an award.

In Galway the most extraordinary circumstances sometimes give rise to actions: a man driving a car along the roadway about twenty miles from his own village saw a dog which he believed to be that of one of his neighbours. Unfortunately he had a few drinks, but out of charity he got out of the car, seized the dog and put it on the seat beside him. The animal was restless and attempted to jump out. To secure him he went to his boot, got a rope and put it around the dog's neck and tied it somewhere in the car. As it was a warm summer night he opened a window. Rounding a corner at a high rate of speed, the dog was flung out and swung from the side of the car like a chair-a-plane in a funfair. The animal was flying along in the air, when he struck a lady pedestrian, causing her injury.

On another occasion, a client whom I had to defend was driving his Volkswagen Beetle car down a hill on a perfectly straight road when he suddenly went out of control. The car crossed the road striking a vehicle travelling in the opposite direction. Asked to explain the accident, the driver said:

'Didn't I have a little bullock on the seat beside me and him strapped in safely by the seat belt? He let a roar out of him, broke the belt and gave me arm a jogging, and sure there was nothing I could do then, except try to steer the best I could.'

One evening at half past seven, Mr Chance, having finished a hard day's work of operating, giving evidence about backs and seeing patients in his surgery, sat down to his dinner in his charming house in Merrion Square. Suddenly his housekeeper rushed in.

'Mr Chance,' she said, 'sir, there's a man in terrible agony out in the hallway, you'll have to come.'

Out on a bench down the hall was a man clutching his stomach and groaning. Concerned, Mr Chance rushed over to him.

'My man, my man what's the matter with you?'

'Oh me bloody stomach it's awful, it's awful.'

'Here,' said Mr Chance, 'undo your vest and let me examine you. Have you received an injury?'

'Oh, I think I have, I think I have. Are you Mr Chance?'

'Of course I am, my good man, I am, I am Mr Chance.'

'Mr Arthur Chance, the famous surgeon?'

'Never mind about that, let's see what's wrong with you.'

'Are you sure,' (groan, moan, sigh) 'are you sure you're Mr Chance?'

'Open your vest, my man.'

'Well then here, Mr Chance, take this', and the man put his hand in his pocket, took out a document and handed it to the doctor. It was a witness subpoena to appear in the Circuit Court in Wicklow on the following morning.

With mounting anger, Mr Chance read the document, while the man fled out the hall door, curses and shouts hurtling past him.

I was briefed by Boyle Fawsett to appear for the workman. The following morning I was in the dingy consultation room at ten o'clock.

'I've been having terrible difficulty with Chance', Boyle informed me. 'He's the only witness we have, except Dr Keaveney here. Dr Keaveney can't help very much, but Mr Chance has said he's pretty bad.'

'Well,' I said, 'is the great man coming down?'

'I served a subpoena on him last night', said Boyle.

The rickety stairs resounded to the tramp of loud footsteps. In came Mr Chance, eyes flashing.

'Where is that so-called solicitor Fawsett?' he said.

'How dare you, sir,' said Boyle, 'refer to me in those terms.'

'You're the man who had a subpoena served on me?'

'I had to, your secretary said you would not come.' There followed a number of gutter swear words, which would be readily written down in a modern novel. Here was this immaculately dressed elderly gentleman, pouring forth obscenities on to the head of the equally elegantly clad Boyle, and the latter responding in like fashion.

Dr Keaveney and I were huddled, meanwhile, in a corner, with our heads bowed in embarrassment, sedulously inspecting the wallpaper as if it were a Miro abstract painting. I turned around at last.

'Look,' I said, 'we're here because Ben Mulligan has a broken knee and can't work. I suggest we forget all this and have a consultation.'

'I'll have no consultation with you, Fawsett', shouted Chance. I thought Boyle would try and throw him out the window.

'Then perhaps you might have a consultation with me?'

'Yes I will, MacKenzie, but not in the presence of Fawsett.'

'I forbid you, MacKenzie, as my counsel, to have a consultation with this doctor without my presence. I will not countenance it.'

And so on. Meantime, I left the room, went down and met my opponent. Previously I had had a consultation with Mulligan, a most amenable man who was quite anxious to get back to work. I got him a lump sum settlement.

Five minutes before the court was due to sit, I arrived back in the consultation room and announced, rather cheekily, I suppose:

'Well boys, you can all go home, I've settled the case, and I've provided a fee of twenty-five guineas for you Mr Chance for your travelling expenses down.'

The great man was somewhat mollified by that, but he didn't wait to partake of the boiled eggs over at The Wicklow.

A virtually unused branch of medicine in the courts was psychiatry. There used to be only two practitioners in Dublin. It was said then that a doctor who failed everything else took to that branch of medicine. Nowadays, when nothing can be found wrong with a client, the solicitor sends him to a psychiatrist who has very little difficulty in finding a traumatic overlay or neurosis which makes imaginary pains real.

The old psychiatrists would get into the witness box and say that despite treatment, a patient would not get well until he had received his damages. This was not in their view a conscious issue for compensation, but a completely genuine condition.

In once such case, Ernest Wood, who was for the defendant, asked the doctor:

'What sort of treatment did you give your patient to cure him of his terrible problems?'

'Well, I kept on reassuring him.'

'What were you reassuring him about?'

'Reassuring him that he was going to get better.'

'And what would make him better, and when?'

'Well, I told him he would certainly be better when he gets his damages.'

'And then, that's your treatment for a man who has had an accident and claims damages, tell him when he gets his money he'll be better?'

'Yes, it is.'

'And what do you do for the fellows who have no claim for damages?'

'What do you mean?'

'Well, you must have clients who are suffering from neurosis, who have no claim for damages.'

'No,' said the doctor, 'I've never had one of those.'

One of the medical men who frequently came to court was a surgeon called 'Pops' Morrin, who was a very distinguished and prominent man in one of the big hospitals. His approach, however, was rather blunt. When a psychiatrist had given the usual evidence about traumatic neurosis he said:

'That man's wife should have beaten him out to work with a stick about three weeks after the accident and we wouldn't all be here wasting our time and the public's money.'

A client of mine in Athy had the craftiness to develop an acute psychiatric problem. He had a very sympathetic doctor who believed in him infinitely. This practitioner, in the witness box, recounted an incident when, happening to be passing by a public house on the main street of the town, and hearing shouts and roars inside and screams for a doctor, he rushed in and saw his patient.

The latter was not peacefully enjoying a drink from his pint of stout but instead he was actually chewing and swallowing the glass.

The jury decided that no lunacy in relation to a pint of stout could be so bad as that and disbelieved him completely.

A poor woman from the Dundalk area was involved in a motor accident. She received facial injuries. She was not very young nor very attractive and the cuts and the abrasions were not really disfiguring. However she had bitten her tongue, and a false tooth had broken and embedded itself there. Of course it was removed, but the wound would not heal. Meeting her in consultation I gathered she was very anxious to settle her case and would practically accept anything. She was a passenger in a motor car, no question of liability arose. It was only a question of amount.

Her doctor was a very well known plastic surgeon and I asked him about her tongue, what could be done for it. He looked at me and said:

'Just one thing, it should be cut out.'

I gasped. 'But why?'

'I think that she's got cancer there in her tongue.'

'But,' I said, 'what a terrible thing it is to have a tongue cut out.'

'Not at all', said the surgeon who could not himself be said to be guilty of much eloquence or diction. 'Not at all, she'll be able to manage very well without it.'

'Will she be able to talk?'

'A little bit, I think, a little bit. Yea, she'll be all right, it will save her life.'

Naturally I said nothing about this to the poor lady, but going to the other side, I informed them of what the surgeon would say. After scoffing for a while, they began to realise the seriousness of the situation, and I got a magnificent offer of settlement, which the amazed lady very gratefully received. Nevertheless, I often thought about her and wondered how she got on when her tongue was amputated.

Eighteen months later, I met my instructing solicitor in another case.

'Do you remember that lady who had the cancerous tongue?'

'Oh, yes, Mrs so and so.'

'Did she ever have the operation to remove her tongue?'

He roared with laughter.

'No, no.'

'Obviously then she's not dead.'

'No, a month after the settlement, she went for a check up to the local G.P. On giving her a routine examination, he discovered she had a mild form of diabetes, easily curable by diet and tablets.'

'And her tongue?'

'Cleared up completely after a few weeks.'

Once a year the Circuit Court used to sit in Baltinglass for one day, presumably to clear up the business from West Wicklow.

By this time I had graduated from a £50 car to a second-hand, prewar Singer sports car, a beautiful vehicle with big silver lamps, copper cylinder head, spotlights, wooden dashboard and a magnificent hood that took about five minutes to get into position. I brought a young barrister down with me.

I had a peculiar case which lasted there all day. My client was a thirty-five-year-old man. When a child, his mother had sent him to live with an uncle, a brother of his father, who was a Protestant, the mother having brought the child up as a Catholic. The uncle had a sheep farm and lived in primitive conditions up in the Glen of Imaal. The young boy did everything, milking, herding, housework and cooking. A pot was kept on the fire and from time to time something was thrown into it, either a turnip or potato or a few rashers of bacon. This young man lived like a recluse. He had never been to a cinema or a dance hall although, as I say, well on in years. He had never been to Dublin or to any other town except Baltinglass and then only two or three times in his life.

The uncle eventually died. He did not honour his promise and will the place to my client, but another nephew of his own religious persuasion.

Unfortunately, the law was against my client and, instead of getting the land, he received only a pittance for the many years of labouring work he had spent on the farm. I believe such cases would not be decided that way now.

Disappointed, we went to the local for a few drinks after the trial was over. The young barrister drank two or three pints of stout. On the way home it was apparent that the hops were having a laxative effect upon him and he asked me to stop the car.

'What am I going to do?' he said. 'I think I'm going to get a terrible attack of the squits.'

'Here,' I said, 'there are some old briefs of mine in the back of the car. They're over and done with, take this one. One of Arthur Chance's reports is there and it's on very soft paper.'

My friend climbed over the fence into the ditch and emerged five minutes later, much relieved.

'I've thrown the brief into the ditch', he said. 'Is that all right?'

'Of course.'

We drove back to town, having some more pints on the way.

An old friend of mine, John Brennan, the principal in the long established firm of Huggard and Brennan of Wexford was sitting in his office one day, surrounded by papers relating to the trusts and settlements of the local gentry in Wexford. His secretary came in.

'Mr Brennan, there's a sergeant of the guards from Wicklow most anxious to see you.'

'To see me?' said John, in some astonishment.

'Yes,' she said, 'it's most important.'

'Well show him in.'

The sergeant came in and saluted.

'Mr Brennan of Huggard and Brennan?' said he.

'Yes indeed, what can I do for you?'

'We have found vital and important documents which we believe emanated from this office and, assuring you of the utmost confidentiality, I beg to return them to you.'

To John's astonishment, he handed him a brief.

It was the one which had been made use of to good purpose and discarded in the ditch near Baltinglass.

It was indeed consoling to know that the members of the Gardaí were so vigilant and on the job.

9

I seldom ventured beyond the Eastern Circuit, but occasionally I went to the neighbouring Midlands and Leinster Circuits. Tom Hannon, Oliver Gogarty and Peter Nugent were the up and coming young men of the Midlands, a hard living, hard drinking establishment. There was also a brilliant performer, who unfortunately died in his prime, Bob Hogan. When on his death bed he was reputed to have said:

'Please God, don't let Kingsmill Moore write my obituary.'

The Eastern and Midland were totally different from the Leinster. The latter was extremely formal. There a Circuit dinner was held every night, presided over by the longest serving barrister, known as the Father. Unpunctuality, or some other breach of convention or etiquette was punished by a fine — usually the presentation of a case of wine. As a result of the fines, the mess in each town had a good collection in the cellar of whatever hotel was used.

The presiding judge in the Midland Circuit was Bill Gleeson, as much a man of the world as anyone appearing before him. I never heard any complaints about his conduct or his decisions except his reluctance to sit late to finish a case. If any proposition was put to him which was unrealistic, or if a witness gave some evidence which could not possibly be believed, he would raise his eyes to the ceiling and say:

'Listen here, do you think I live in the Mo---een?'

For the youthful members of the Bar, recently called, he showed a particular kindness. On learning that a newcomer had arrived on the Circuit, he would come into court, look around him and fix his eye on a bashful youth with astonishment.

'Mr ---,' he would say, 'it is a surprise to see you here and a great pleasure for me and I heartily welcome you. I have followed your brilliant career at the University and at the King's Inns. I was hoping, but I did not think, that you would select this Circuit, having seen how well you were progressing. I am glad you are here, I am glad you are practising in the Midlands. I am sure you will be a great success and I wish you very well.'

At least to have your name announced in court prior to

travelling from town to town, sitting behind the established juniors, hoping for work, always seemed a conspicuous send off for a young man.

On occasions when in a hurry, on a case being called, Tom Hannon would open the facts to the judge.

'Is that what you say then, Mr Hannon?' he would say and then he would look at Nugent.

'What do you say to that, Pether?'

'My client completely disagrees.' He would then recite the defence for the case.

'Very well then, I know all about it, can I decide on your opening statements?'

Although the parties were entitled to twelve good men and true, using juries in the Circuit Court fell into disuse. The idea was disliked by the judges, and as the cases were afterwards reheard before a High Court Judge, the use of the jury was superfluous. Occasionally a plaintiff would demand one, and the whole rigmarole would have to be gone through, summoning of a panel and the selection of the twelve rate-payers of £20 valuation.

The last jury trial on that Circuit was brought by a man who claimed to be a connoisseur of Guinness' extra stout. He had gone to a new public house, ordered a large pint bottle and was about to enjoy it. As he drank the first sip, he noticed something strange floating on the top of the pint — a dead mouse. Dramatically and with a shout, he threw the pint down on the ground and proceeded to be ill. These cases are common since 1932 when Mrs Donaghue went to a café in Scotland to consume ice cream in a tumbler with ginger beer poured over it, and a decomposed snail emerged from the ginger beer bottle as it was being poured on the ice cream, Mrs Donaghue suffered shock and severe gastroenteritis and she successfully recovered against the manufacturer of the beverage. Since then worms have turned up in jam pots, teeth in bread, nails in buns — a barrel of pigs' heads was once reputed to have contained a human skull — giving rise to many actions, some successful, others not so.

The male jury appeared to be pint or large bottle of stout drinkers to a man. The plaintiff's case was opened with a statement that irreparable physical damage had been suffered. His stomach was always aching, he had headaches, lack of energy and his enjoyment of life was gone.

Guinness was his real enjoyment, large bottles of stout, and here the bottler, the reckless publican, had allowed a dead mouse to enter during the filling process. Whether the mouse was drowned by the stout, or dead sober on entry was immaterial. What else was there left to a working man nowadays, but his pint and his smoke?

Noll Gogarty, who was appearing for the defendant, listened rather gloomily, seeing the indignation on the face of the jury.

The plaintiff having described his illness, stomach upset, headaches, nausea, proceeded to describe his next purchase of a bottle of stout.

'It was poured out,' he said, 'but I've got myself — and it was as a result of what happened — in such a terrible condition that I couldn't have faced it. If a pint of stout or a large bottle of stout was placed before me, it had this most awful terrible, terrible effect on me.'

'Tell us then,' said his counsel, 'what effect had it?'

'Well it's like this, yer Honour,' he looked up at the judge and looked at the jury, 'it's just like this, every time I see a bottle of stout before me, what do I think of, would you believe it? I can see and think of nothing but a mouse and what's worse, sometimes instead of seeing a lovely bottle of stout, there I am looking at a mouse. A bottle of stout always appears as a mouse to me.'

The shocked jury exchanged murmurs of sympathy. Rising in his stately presence, Noll Gogarty looked at him for a while.

'Tell me my good man,' he said, 'aren't you extremely lucky?'

'Lucky? Why do you say that?'

'It's a mouse you see instead of a bottle of stout, isn't that right?'

'Yes.'

'Isn't it the case, then, that every time you see a mouse, you see a bottle of stout?'

He sat down, the man's case was thrown out. It was heard afterwards that the plaintiff had slipped the mouse in himself.

Harry Whelahan who went on the Midland as a junior brought me a letter recently which had been given to him by a client.

'This is the cure, Pat', he said. 'I have it especially for yourself and Ernest Wood.

I quote the letter in full:

> *Cacracandra,*
> *Swinford,*
> *Co. Mayo.*

Dear Mr Whelahan,

Hope you remember me, Margaret Byrne, from the High Court in Galway, last March.
I said if you got me the money, I would cure your baldness.
I got your address from Mr John O'Connor for this purpose last May. I've been putting it off, but it always kept nagging at the back of my mind, so here goes.
Cut an onion in two, soak it in a little rum overnight, rub the cut onion in circular movements over the scalp night and morning. Cut surface off onion after use, thrust back into rum. Renew after a few days. Should see results after three months.

Thanking you for all you did for me,

Yours sincerely,

Margaret Byrne.

It proved to be a terrible waste of rum — and onion.

For his retirement, a great dinner was organised by all the Circuit for Bill Gleeson. A presentation was considered to be appropriate, and Seán Gannon, who was the junior at that time, was deputed to organise the gift. He consulted the judge in his room as to what he, the judge, thought would be appropriate.

'Bedad, I think it should be something special', said Bill.

'Of course.' Seán was thinking of a set of Waterford glass.

'Me car is pretty beat up by now, it would be a very fitting gesture, I think, if I were to get a new one.'

Sometimes jaws drop when people suffer shock. Seán's almost fell to his chest.

A reasonable car in those days was priced at about £400. By cajoling all the solicitors, running a sweep on the Grand National,

Seán managed to raise the money. A large number attended the dinner. The hotels in Mullingar were booked out. A set of keys was ceremoniously presented to the judge.

In the early hours of the morning following the banquet, Tom Hannon made his way to the hotel. The night porter was on duty. Tom's key was not in its pigeon hole, No. 16, nor was it in his pocket.

'It's No. 16,' said Tom, 'I know that.'

'I don't know where it's gone, Mr Hannon, are you sure it's not on you?'

Tom fumbled around.

'I seem to have lost it', he said. 'Have you got a master key that will open all the rooms?'

'Indeed I have sir,' said the porter, 'here, take it, this will get you in anywhere. No. 16 is on the second floor.'

Taking the key he mounted the stairs to the second floor. With difficulty he opened the door of No. 16, turned on the light and was about to throw his clothes on the floor when piercing and resounding screams echoed throughout the hotel. A lady was sitting up in the bed, clutching the sheet to her chest, screaming and shouting for help.

'What are you up to you, you brute?'

'My bedroom...' said Tom.

'Go out you, go out you...!'

Tom backed away. Sixteen was the number of his bedroom certainly — but unfortunately it was in the only other hotel in the town.

In that hostelry, Peter Nugent decided that a really hot bath would be most refreshing and would help to sober him up. Filling the tub he sighed and flopped in with the steaming water up to his chin. Five hours later, he woke petrified in freezing water. He was lucky to survive.

If you practise on a Circuit long enough, some clients come again and again. Tom Finlay, who had an enormous practice there, had such a client. This man was stopped by the Gardaí one night, who accused him of dangerous driving and incapacity due to the consumption of alcohol. He was smelling very strongly of drink. They arrested him and asked him to come to the station, where he would be formally charged. He managed to mount the steps of

Athlone barracks without stumbling too much and was brought into the only cell to await the arrival of a medical practitioner, who would conduct an examination as to his capacity or incapacity to drive. In the cell Tom's client sat despondently on the bunk and looked around him. It was gloomy and chilly. Three bottles of milk reclined on the window ledge. Seizing upon them, despite his revulsion, in half an hour he managed demolish all three, an especially difficult feat as he had not drunk milk since childhood. He placed the empty bottles under the bunk. The sergeant came in and announced the arrival of the doctor. By this time the milk was beginning to react. The prisoner was alert and probably sober. After a five minute examination, the doctor went back to the sergeant and informed him that a mistake had been made. The accused man was completely free from the effects of alcohol and quite capable of driving a double-decker bus, if necessary. Why was he called out needlessly? In annoyance, the doctor departed.

The sergeant shook his prisoner by the hand, tore up the charge sheet and gave him the car keys, saying:

'Now sir, before you start on your journey, Garda Cullen here will make us all a nice cup of tea.'

'I'd rather be on my way.'

'No, it would be much better for you, warm you up on this cold night.'

They sat down, the cups were set out, the tea made.

'Get the milk now', said the sergeant.

Garda Cullen departed and came back a few minutes later.

'Sergeant, there isn't any milk.'

'Why isn't there?'

'I don't know. I thought I'd left it at the window, it's not there now.'

'You forgot it, that's what you did, you forgot it. The only thing you have to do in this station down here is to see that there's milk for the tea and now we have none. What sort of an eejit are you?'

'I'm frightfully sorry, sir,' he said to Tom's client, 'only for this *amadán* we could set you off warm on your journey with a nice hot cup of tea.'

'Not at all, not at all, I'll readily drink the tea without any milk, with sugar only, don't blame the poor Garda.'

10

On the last day of the autumn term, usually about 21 December, the Leinster Bar held, and still hold, their annual dinner.

The venue used to be the upstairs room in Jammets, with the window overlooking the Provost's Gardens in Trinity College. Now the spectator can see one of Ireland's most hideous buildings. They were lavish in the number of guests they had, inviting any judge who had any association with the Circuit, including those who during the year had tried the appeals. There might be sometimes eight members of the judiciary present, drinking the best of wine and eating the best of food at the expense of the young members of the Circuit who could not consist of more than twelve or fifteen practitioners. I always thought this most unfair, some people then were earning very little money.

By custom, the speech in honour of the guests was made by the youngest barrister, usually the probationer. At his first dinner when James Skinner had been two months called to the Bar, it was his task to make the welcoming speech to what RTE would call the dignitaries and honoured guests.

The judicial invitees were seated at the top table in various states of self importance and inebriety. The 'father' of the Circuit presided.

'I am looking around me,' began Jim Skinner, 'I see with horror what I might become in my old age, one of those festooning the father in their positions as honoured and learned guests.

'Let me tell you a story, if I may.

'Two explorers were walking along the banks of the Nile. To avoid trampling on a rattle snake, one jumped aside but unfortunately fell into the river.

'"Are you all right?" said the one still on the bank, "Are you all right?"

'"Be God I'm right enough," said the one in the river, "I've escaped the snake but to tell you the truth, I'm afraid I'm up to my arse in crocodiles."'

Jim paused, the joke brought very few sniggers.

'But by analogy,' continued Jim, 'I'll tell you tonight I feel like that explorer in the river, except that I'm up to my arse in judges.'

There was uproar and pandemonium. The young members of the Circuit rolled in the aisles, some of the judges smiled, others not.

Tom Bacon, the father of the Bar, his face puce with rage, rose to his feet, shouting:

'How dare you sir, how dare you sir? I suggest you leave this dinner.'

The cheers of the younger set drowned his voice. There was no question of Jim having to beat a retreat. He afterwards became Chief Justice in one of the emerging African states.

At the beginning of my third year in practice, when the leaves were falling on an autumn day, I sat in a gleaming new Armstrong Sidley car. A wealthy solicitor was driving me down to the town of Rathdowney, in County Laois. A Commission had been appointed to take the evidence of my client, who was too incapacitated to leave hospital and travel to the High Court in Dublin. With the solicitor showing off his driving and terrifying me, we arrived at the hotel for lunch at one o'clock. The Commission was to take place in the afternoon when my client would give evidence, on oath, and his testimony would be taken down. It was a balmy day in early October and the sun shone as it might in August.

The defendant was the Electricity Supply Board, whose van had struck my client on a crossroads outside the town. It was doubtful whether his present incapacity was due to that accident or not, but he had sustained injuries. However, the case we were trying to make suggested the accident had precipitated his condition of complete immobility.

The ESB were insured by a Lloyd's syndicate and a very posh team was assembled against us. They had Senior and Junior Counsel, a prominent solicitor and also the man from Lloyd's, bowler hat and all.

Down at the nursing home we met our client, a former British Army captain. He was a member of a prominent brewing family in that area. He was lying in bed and smiled warmly and shook our hands. He was a really gentle, elderly man, but he could not speak. In answer to questions, he nodded and grunted, but could not articulate.

This was a difficult situation. The first row erupted when the plaintiff endeavoured to take the oath. Eventually the Commissioner was persuaded that his nod and grunt at the end of the words of affirmation were sufficient and the business of taking the evidence started. There were strong rejections from the great man.

'Were you on 4 October driving your motor car at a place called Golshia Cross?' I began.

Grunt.

'Did you have a collision there with an ESB van?'

Grunt.

The posh senior bristled. 'I'm objecting to all this on the basis that these questions are leading questions and further this witness does not answer them. He makes a noise which could mean anything.'

'I propose to bring this man through his evidence in this fashion,' I said 'by asking him leading questions, and to get the Commissioner to note that his answers to these are in the affirmative or in the negative. I'm asking him to nod or shake his head.'

A big fuss ensued. The Lloyd's man, the Lloyd's solicitor, Senior and Junior Counsel went out and paced up and down the corridor. I had told them if they did not wish to partake in the Commission I would go ahead myself.

They came back, I proceeded somewhat as follows:

'Did you see a van coming down a side road?'

Grunt, nod.

'Did you see it travelling at a very high speed?' 'Did it come through the crossroads without stopping?' 'Did it strike you while you were stationary?' and 'Were you hurt in the accident?' 'Was it in any way your fault?' And so on.

We did not part in friendly circumstances. The rich solicitor and I went to see the local doctor, who, pouring us out two enormous glasses of Irish whiskey, warned us that it was unlikely that the poor patient would survive very long.

Feeling not very optimistic, but fairly elated at the excitement of the whole thing, we sped home in the Armstrong Sidley.

Next morning in the Library I was approached by the ESB counsel who made me an offer of settlement on condition that the plaintiff was alive that very hour, which was eleven o'clock.

Taking instructions from my solicitors, rapidly despite the

appalling telephone service, he told me to jump at it.

We settled at 11.30.

The poor man died at twelve noon.

The least worried was the man from Lloyd's who was waiting outside the Library door. He asked me to have a cup of coffee.

In the restaurant he said, 'The ESB have an important Circuit Court appeal in two weeks time in Carlow, our junior has now taken silk, we would be very glad if you would handle it for us.'

Naturally I was delighted.

The defendant's case was simple: they were repairing an electricity pole on the side of the road; the equipment was in a van which was parked on a corner; it being in the heart of the country, there was no traffic; it was perfectly visible, but the plaintiff, a lady on her bicycle, struck the van and injured herself. We ought to hold the dismissal of her case by the Circuit Court Judge. Cecil Lavery was the Appeal Judge.

Ours was the first of a number of cases on that day and the court was crowded. The plaintiff, a middle-aged, plump rustic woman of about thirty, said, 'I got on me bicycle to go to the village of Cretyard to buy some tea and sugar. I was cycling along not too hard, not too slow — just nice.'

Whereupon a man at the back of the court clapped his hands and shouted, 'Fair enough!'

'Who said that?' shouted Lavery, but nobody responded.

Approaching a crossroads and near the mouth of the main road an ESB van pulled up in front of her. She could not avoid it. There was a collision. She hurt her wrist, her leg and her head.

I cross-examined her.

'Did you not come down a steep hill, Madam?'

'Ah, a bit of a hill.'

'And wasn't the ESB van parked there all the time, for half an hour before you arrived?'

'Not to my knowledge, I only saw it at the last moment.'

'Isn't that the truth of it, you weren't watching out? And furthermore, didn't you come speeding down the hill, shouting "I have no brakes, I have no brakes, get that bloody van out of the way as quick as you can"?'

'Not at all, not at all.'

'And didn't you bang into it when it was stationary?'

The lady denied all this. Five ESB workmen swore that this

was what happened.

Cecil Lavery said in his judgment that it was quite disgraceful that people like the ESB should park their motor vans at a cross roads, in the manner that they did, where an unfortunate lady like the plaintiff, cycling on her bicycle, with admittedly quite defective brakes, would be completely obstructed and so injured. He gave her a decree.

I learned afterwards that two days previously, the judge having forgotten to pay his electricity bill, the company had cut off his supply.

11

The Dublin Circuit was dominated by George Shannon who became the first President of the Circuit Court. A man of great ability, but disappointed that he was not a High Court Judge. He was one of the State's earliest appointments, together with Cahir Davitt, who later became President of the High Court. Then only two Circuit Courts sat in Dublin. So little work was there that it was easily disposed of. Now there are eight judges.

An astounding snob, George constantly wriggled his nose and sniffed in distaste at any person who happened to come into his disfavour. Such people were of what he regarded as the lower orders. Although malicious, he tried cases well, knew everything about the law, but was extremely aloof.

In modern parlance, he put down as many barristers as he could with his sarcasm. While being abrupt with practitioners, he was invariably smarmily polite to witnesses, particularly if they were what he would have considered his social equals.

John Cassidy told me he was conducting a case as carefully and peacefully as he could when a bellow came from George:

'Mr Cassidy, you are a disgrace to your profession.'

John was flabbergasted.

'Why, why? What have I done? Why do you say that, my Lord?'

'You are a positive disgrace.'

'But why, m'Lord?'

'Your braces are showing.'

A requirement of the Bar, more honoured in the breach at present, is that a junior should wear a waistcoat.

On one occasion, a civil action having taken the whole of the previous day, it was due to recommence immediately after the morning list was called over. One counsel, anxious to have his witnesses attend on time (this was a rule upon which Shannon always insisted — he would wait for nobody), mentioned that he had been informed by Mr Cherry, who was engaged in the case at hearing, that it would occupy most of the day.

Shannon sniffed and, wrinkling his nose, said, 'I can assure you that it will take nothing like that, so you better be prepared to go on with your case at any time.'

Richard Cherry stood up.

'It is my opinion,' he said, 'my case will take probably the whole day, but it is obvious that your Lordship thinks you know more about it than I do, but as far as I am concerned, if it is to be done properly, it will occupy all the time available.'

He sat down.

George Shannon became red with fury, but could say nothing.

After Cahir Davitt moved on, in the second court across the corridor, a totally different character presided, Judge Martin Connolly.

He was a very grand person. Originating from Roundstone in the west of Ireland, but never practising in that area, attaching himself to the Leinster Circuit. By great diligence and perseverance he built up a great business. He failed to fulfil his promise, however, on taking silk. He too was a snob and fancied himself as a great gentleman. In ejectment cases it was his delight to announce to Judge Sealy on the Leinster Circuit, that he appeared for his landlord and his friend appeared for the 'tinnent'.

Martin Connolly carefully and painstakingly prepared his opening statements. Explaining the circumstances and facts in a Malicious Injury Claim which occurred in a certain place in Tipperary, the judge interrupted and said:

'Ah Mr Connolly, is that place not the scene of that great novel by Charles Kickham, *Knocknagow*?' To which Martin explained impatiently:

'If you had allowed me m'Lord, I was coming to that.'

He had a dry sense of humour. He disliked George Shannon as much as anybody else and continually referred to him as 'the man in the hard hat'.

One day a lady appearing before him in an ejectment case said to him that she was a poor widow. Martin looked at her.

'I know you are a widow', he said. Then, with a burst of craftiness: 'At least so you tell me. But even tho' you are a widow, you must pay your rint as tho' you were a spinster.'

In a sexual case, a girl complained that the man had

overpowered her by putting her legs into strap hangers which were a feature of old-fashioned cars for the convenience of passengers to cling to as they swayed around corners.

Martin looked at the ceiling and sniffed.

'I always wondered what those things were there for', he said.

Martin had an usher called Bill Keenan, who became a famous character around the courts. Every day the judge lunched on a boiled egg, but his egg had to be cooked to a certain consistency. Keenan used to bring it to him from the restaurant. To have it boiled on a stove in the Chamber must have been too much for Keenan's culinary expertise.

The egg not being to his liking on one occasion, he flung it up in the air, where it stuck to the ceiling. Bespotted by bluebottles it remained there for many weeks.

Keenan was a personality in his own right. Before he found his way into the Four Courts, he was a barman in Downey's Public House in Dún Laoghaire.

On the retirement of his judge, an usher is always in a dilemma. He has to find another position. His job with Martin did not involve driving, and the judge's successor required someone who could drive a motor vehicle, which Keenan could not. He was a strong political man, however, and eventually became the Chief Porter in the Round Hall, otherwise known as an Admiral, with a magnificent hat and uniform full of gold braid. His partner at that time was another ex-crier, called Berry. Together these two animated and lit up the building, literally and figuratively speaking, for they made no secret of their fondness of Power's whiskey.

After some time I began to get business from insurance companies and became friendly with Ernest Wood, an astute performer and a feared cross-examiner. Although they have full managerial staffs in Ireland, an English insurance company, when they have an important, or so-called important, case, send over an official from the Head Office claims department, on the basis that their competence in handling claims far exceeds the most clever Irish manager. Of course it was a holiday outing for the man from Head Office.

Before one such case, a consultation was held in the evening with the witnesses and the London man. The defence case on liability was a sorry one and, having talked about the facts for an hour, we all agreed that it was hopeless and that a settlement, if possible, should be effected.

'What do you say, Mr Wood?' asked the London man.

Ernest said he thought it could be bought off.

'Why do you say that?'

'I know my opponent has put a value on it. It's quite moderate.'

'How much, Mr Wood?'

Ernest mentioned the figure.

'Upon my soul, Mr Wood, upon my soul, I wouldn't dream of it. My company would never pay such a figure. It's outrageous, I'd be laughed out of London. My underwriters would never stop sneering.'

'Maybe, but you'll be laughed out of Dublin if you don't jump at it.'

'I'll tell you, I'm not expecting to pay even half of that sum.'

'Very well, we'll fight the case for you.'

'That's just what I expect my counsel to do, go in and do battle. I want you to get me a good result.'

'You're missing an opportunity', said Wood.

Next morning the Round Hall, as I recollect, was thronged. The noise was well beyond the usual bustle, commensurate with the sound emanating from the Paris Bourse, during a heavy trading session. People pushed, shouted, shoved and were shoved. It was then, and still is, a bewildering place for litigants, but more so in the days of the jury trials.

Our case was designated to Court No. 4, not a particularly happy one for plaintiffs at that time.

In the midst of it all, looking slightly incongruous was the London man, with a bowler hat, black coat, striped trousers and a rolled umbrella, dressed for the City.

We were standing outside the court waiting for the case to commence. He gave a diffident cough.

'Mr Wood, I say Mr Wood, do you think you can do something to settle the case?'

'I can try, but certainly not for the money you were thinking of last night. Far too low. This case is worth much more than you think. I know we've got a good judge.'

'But you mentioned a figure at the consultation that you said the other side would be interested in. Could you effect a settlement about that figure. Is it available?'

'I can try.'

The thought of the judge in Court No. 4 was unnerving the plaintiffs. A good settlement was effected, below the sum mentioned the evening before.

Any visitor to our shores was entitled to a little hospitality and, after a couple of gins and tonics in Annie's Bar, we went off to lunch to the old Dolphin.

While we were awaiting the delicious steaks being cooked before our eyes in the Grill Room, Ernest said to the London man, 'Will you tell me one thing please before we start our lunch and stop talking about law and cases. Last evening you were adamant that you wouldn't settle, that you wanted to fight, that you wouldn't pay the money. What made you change your mind?'

'I'll tell you, it's like this, Mr Wood. Here was I in that great big Round Hall, a stranger far from home, like Ruth amidst the alien corn, cast like one in the wilderness.'

'Hardly an accurate analogy, but I see your point.'

'I saw a great, red-faced man, dressed up in a uniform with lots of gold braid upon it and a gold sailor's hat.'

'Keenan, the porter.'

'I know he was the chief porter.'

'What about him?'

'You said, "Good morning Keenan." He came up to you — my leading Q.C. — put his arm around your shoulder and said, "'Ow is the 'ead today Hearnest?" I realised then I was in a different country, far from home and I'd better conform to local custom.'

12

A prominent firm of engineers was employed at the deepening of the docks in Galway, a seabed of rock had to be blasted away. During several of the explosions rocks flew through the air damaging nearby buildings and smaller particles and stones landed on the streets of the city. An action was brought by a warehouse man, whose premises were close to the dock, for damages to the buildings, caused by negligence and nuisance.

Peter Maguire and I were employed to defend the action.

The insurance company was full of fight. Experts came in from all parts of the globe to testify as to the soundness of the 'orthodox' methods employed by the defendants to control the effects of the blasting. They would not hear of criticism.

After a second long consultation, Peter said, 'By the way, did you notice the hands of our explosion experts?'

Like Doctor Watson, who paid no attention to the curious failure of a dog bark, in one of the Sherlock Holmes stories, I had not observed. At the next consultation I looked: few of the experts had any fingers left.

The case of course had to settle, but the London man resisted until the door of Galway Courthouse. He got a satisfactory discount on the claim and we all went down to the Tavern, an excellent restaurant in Eyre Square, which was too good to last.

The Tavern was on a par with the Oyster in Cork, which in turn resembled the Dolphin Hotel in Dublin. These are places never written up by the brigade of writers who commence dinner with garlic mushrooms, eat crispy chunky vegetables and lovely garlicky prawns and who don't seem ever to have downed a good, non sauced, sirloin steak.

The London man, a little chap, did not appear to be enjoying himself. He seemed to be nervous and worried about something.

The case had been expected to last for four days and he had made the appropriate arrangements, was he now to go home? We suggested that he hire a car and explore the glories of the west of Ireland. His head office would approve.

'I should be home. What would my wife say if she found out?' he said.

'Tell her nothing,' said Peter, 'just go.'
'Ah, but the day after tomorrow is Thursday', said he.
'What's that got to do with it?'
'My wife goes to bridge that night.'
'So what?'
'I'm expected to babysit.'
'But you said you'd no children.'
'I know — she makes me babysit for the cat.'

The only solicitor who ever gave me a brief in County Meath was the late Nat Lacy. He had an enormous practice, afterwards spreading his office into Dublin. The first case we had together involved a girl, who claimed that while working as a nanny, she pricked her finger with a knitting needle, developing an infection. We thought it was so improbable an accident — she could have picked up the infection anywhere, at weekends at home, on her evenings off and a thousand other places besides where she worked. The insurance company was so indignant that we were given demonstrations in knitting to be able to argue that no knitting needle could prick and wound a finger. After she had won, the case even went to the Supreme Court, which affirmed her award.

Not only was Nat an able and successful solicitor, but he was a fearless and lucky punter. The only person I've ever met who was able, year in year out, to attend practically every race meeting in the immediate vicinity of Dublin and survive. He brought off some great coups and never minded giving his tips and information to others.

He told me about a case he had, also in Galway city, where the insurance man from London had arrived to supervise personally. What he would make of the jury system in Galway and the Galway courthouse, with a witness sitting on a chair, perched on a table in front of the judge and the jury in a box so high up in the air that they could not be seen or see, some of whom had come from the Aran Islands and could not speak English, can only be guessed.

The Railway Hotel in Eyre Square was the fashionable place to stay during the Sessions. About half a mile or so from the courthouse, Nat and the London man decided to walk. They reached a magnificent building with a pillared portico.

'Excuse me', Nat said and went inside for a minute, leaving his companion on the steps. He emerged a few minutes later.

'Is this not the courthouse?' he was asked.

'No, not at all, it's further on. This is the Franciscan Friary.'

'What did you go in there for, Nat?'

'To offer up a prayer for the success of the Phoenix Insurance Company today.'

'What?'

'I said a little prayer for the company's success.'

'I hope then, you got through to head office quicker than I can.'

Knowing Nat, I'm sure they were successful.

Bob Pellissier at one time managed the Railway Passengers' Insurance Company — what a glorious Victorian name — a company which after several amalgamations ended up in the Hibernian Insurance Company Group.

Very polite, dapper and gentlemanly, he drove down to Kilkenny one time to see a plaintiff's solicitor and endeavour to settle a case. He found himself in the office of a great eccentric, named O'Hanrahan, whose brother was prominent at the Bar and a little unusual himself.

No secretary, no typist, no book-keeper was employed by Mr O'Hanrahan. Everything he did, he did himself and he was not the only solicitor like that in the country. Nothing happened when Bob knocked. Opening the door, he found himself in a room with a counter on the far side of which Mr O'Hanrahan was hammering away at a typewriter. Bob coughed. The solicitor looked up.

'Good day to yeh.'

'I'm from the Hibernian Insurance Company.'

'Yeah.'

'I've come about the case you have with us, O'Loughlin and Newgrange Construction. A claim of a man who was injured at work.'

'Yeah.'

'I want to settle it with you if I can.'

'Yeah.'

There was a pause, nothing seemed to be happening. The typewriter hammered away.

'Can I make you an offer of settlement then?'
The typewriter stopped for a moment. 'Yeah, how much?'
Bob mentioned a figure, much less than the case was worth.
No notice was taken and the typewriting resumed.
Bob coughed after a while and said. 'Well what do you say
about the offer?'
The typewriter continued. Bob coughed again.
'What about the offer?'
The typing stopped, the man looked at him.
'Fuck off', he said.
That was the end of the negotiations.

An old friend of mine, a prominent claims man, who did most of
his work out and about rather than in the office, and did so most
effectively, was put out when his company purchased a computer.
I suppose for these instruments to work, somebody has to put the
data in, and this my friend was expected to do.

He retired, therefore, before his time was up. Coincidentally
with his retirement, a large English firm of loss adjusters opened a
new office in Dublin — they were looking for a manager. This
would be ideal for my friend.

To interview my friend the proprietor of the English firm
came to Dublin. He was given an excellent lunch, after which my
friend suggested that for an hour or so a little drive around Dublin
would be an interesting experience. This was readily agreed.

'I'll show you the Phoenix Park, the largest in Europe.'

He drove around the Park rather slowly and eventually at half
past three arrived near Áras an Uachtaráin.

'What's that fine building over there flying the Irish flag?' the
English man asked.

'Oh, that's known as the Vice Regal Lodge, it's where the
President of Ireland resides.'

'The President of Ireland?'

'Yes, he's the Head of State, equivalent to your Queen. He has
all sorts of constitutional duties.'

'Well, I never knew that, who is he?'

'His name is Erskine Childers, a very prominent and much
respected man. Hey listen, would you like to meet our President?'

'Meet your President, I certainly would! How could it be
arranged?'

'No difficulty at all, no difficulty.'

'Well, I suppose it will have to be at a general audience or something like that. It's very hard to meet our Queen.'

'Not as far as I'm concerned.' My friend turned his motor car, drove down the avenue leading to the gates of the President's house. At the gate the guard saluted. My friend leaned out the window of his car.

'I'm Mr X and I want to see the President.'

'Of course, sir', said the guard. 'He's always delighted to meet you.'

The gates automatically opened. They drove up the avenue, stopped at the steps of the magnificent house. The door opened and President Erskine Childers emerged.

He shook my friend by the hand said, 'Hallo Seán, delighted to see you. Who is your friend?'

Seán introduced the perplexed and bemused Englishman.

'Come in, come in, I'm very busy, but I have time for a little chat and a glass of wine with you.'

The visit lasted a quarter of an hour. Seán got the job.

How was it done? It was a most glorious fix. My friend knew Erskine Childers' election agent from Cavan. He had arranged the visit in advance, specifying the exact time it was to take place and the exact duration. Erskine Childers came up trumps.

13

The most difficult judicial office is that of a District Justice. He has to make up his mind about one thing or another about a hundred times a day. He has constantly to deliver oral decisions and ask questions to clarify the evidence; this is exhausting.

Judges in the higher courts need not say anything except when they are making a ruling or giving a judgment. Whereas one cannot be sympathetic towards blackguards, who steal from, beat and rob old people, there is a constant stream of petty criminals, non-violent and pathetic people who come up repeatedly before the courts. Most of their lives are spent in prison. It is heart-breaking for a justice to see no sign of any reformation in these poor people.

The justice who has charge of Court No. 1 in the Bridewell has to deal with cases expeditiously, as there are so many. Walter Maloney presided there for many years with great success.

When one middle-aged, chronic thief came before him and pleaded guilty, he asked the prisoner had he anything to say.

The man looked at him. 'Well there is nothing I can say at all, except can I ask if it will do any good to say I'm sorry?'

'Words of repentance are like gold and silver', Walter Maloney said. 'Instead of nine months I'll give you six weeks.'

This man had over twenty convictions.

Bob O'Huadhaigh, a contemporary of mine, was appointed a justice in Donegal. Eventually he came back to Dublin and succeeded Walter. He also held his court on a tight rein, but he was constantly reported in the paper by a journalist in such a fashion as to conceal the humanitarian and humorous side of his character.

For any judge the most unnerving and irritating thing to put up with in court is noise, whispers, snuffling, sniffing and coughing. What can one do?

One day, having put up with a great deal of irritating disturbances, Bob nearly blew up when he saw a man chewing gum in the back of the court, nor was he moving his jaws silently, but making great sucking noises. Unable to stand it any longer,

Bob called the elderly Garda, who was a custodian of the court. He approached the bench.

'Yes, Justice.'

'Do you see that man there, third from the end, in the second last bench, wearing a grey jacket?'

The Garda looked down. 'I do, your Honour.'

'Well get down there quickly and tell him to stop masticating.'

A blank uncomprehending look appeared on the face of the Garda. Nevertheless, he made his way to the back of the court, touched the man on the shoulder and said in a loud whisper, 'The justice says, take your hands out of your pockets and keep them out.'

In the courts on the outskirts of the city, like Kilmainham, sometimes even as far as Newbridge in Kildare, sat Kenneth Reddin. He was one of the earliest appointments of the State. A literary man and habitué of the salons where Yeats and A.E. declaimed and the drawing-rooms of Fitzwilliam Square, he wrote two novels, *Somewhere to the Sea* and *Another Shore.*

After one drunken brawl and a ferocious amount of insults to the police, Brendan Behan was hauled before him.

'I was only trying to get the bus to Dún Laoghaire, yer Honour,' said Behan, 'to go to somewhere to the sea, but the Gardaí landed me up on another shore.'

Reddin was delighted, gave a judgment praising Brendan's works, of course letting him off.

He designed a uniform for District Justices. As the only one who ever wore that costume, he had great dignity. He had head gear which looked like that worn by Peter O'Toole in *Lawrence of Arabia,* and a black robe which buttoned up like a priest's soutane. He seldom sat before twelve o'clock, so little work there was then that he easily finished early in the afternoon. He expected solicitors to wear gowns in court and barristers to haul their outfits around to places like Rathfarnham, where the courthouse was so small, they could only robe themselves out on the street. If you failed to accord with the dignity of the administration of justice in his court, Kenneth gave you a pretty bad hearing.

The old *Evening Mail* was the great paper for reporting proceedings in District Courts. The journalists loved Kenneth's philosophical comments and observations on the life and times of the emerging State. He was quoted each evening in that journal. He was a ferocious supporter of the prosecution. Super-intendents of the Gardaí always took lunch in his room, all eating their sandwiches together and giving the justice their opinion as to the guilt or innocence of those accused, mostly guilt. Two of my clients got this treatment with very little evidence against them.

A schoolboy, whose bicycle happened to be parked leaning against a shop window, was accused of stealing a lady's purse. It had been removed from her shopping bag while she was inside making a purchase. The child wasn't even on the premises but, nevertheless, Reddin berated him as a lying little scoundrel and a little thief: no doubt he had heard from the prosecutor that the boy may have had a bad type for a father. I got him off on appeal.

In the other case, a girl who was a telephonist had been asked by a young man to go to a dance one evening. Not having any suitable stockings, she went down to the local shop where she was well known. She waited at the counter but the owner did not come. My client saw the lady proprietor in the sitting-room at the back of the shop, where she was listening to a religious programme on the wireless. She shouted that she was taking two pairs of stockings and would pay for them later. She was in a hurry and could not wait. She took the stockings and innocently went off about her way and enjoyed the dance.

Next morning the Gardaí came to her house and charged her with stealing. She came before Reddin who, to my astonishment, convicted.

A great friend of Reddin was a barrister called Tynan O'Mahony, a little man who was not a member of the Law Library and who had an obvious drink problem. Each evening the *Mail* reported pleasantries exchanged between Mr Tynan O'Mahony and the justice. O'Mahony always carried a little dog and used to stand outside the Law Library with the creature under his arm, asking his colleagues for something to buy the little creature dinner.

Nick Barron was a middle-aged man who was called to the Bar a year after I was. He was born in California of American parents and had a law degree in that State. To escape matrimonial problems he came to Ireland. His uncle was a bishop and got Nick a job as a newscaster in the emerging Radio Athlone. As this task was performed only at six in the evening and nine o'clock in the night, he had spare time on his hands, and was called to the Bar. His legal degree in America did him well as he spent his time drafting affidavits setting out the law in various American States for the administration of assets of a deceased person in that country. With pride he told me he got eight guineas per affidavit. He constantly referred with great pride and joy to 'my uncle Michael, the Bishop'. These inspiring words were introduced into every conversation.

After a few years he was appointed a District Justice.

Those whom the gods wished to destroy they first made mad. Nick Bannon's appointment was temporary for one year, after which he would be made a permanent judicial officer. He had not been sitting more than three months when he read out the Bishop of Galway from the bench, as sometimes the old fashioned priests read parishioners out from the altar or pulpit.

In an application for a Dance Licence he was told that the bishop had written a letter to each Parish Priest stating the hours which, in his view, should be allowed in each dance hall for dancing, essentially ceasing at midnight.

'The boys and girls of Ireland', thundered Nick, 'are not going to be dictated to by the likes of the bishops. They should mind their own business, pray for the dead and dying and let their young flock carry on in the best tradition of the Kerry dancers — and the old Gaelic customs of love, life and laughter. This court will not tolerate interference from clerics.'

The temporary appointment of the bishop's nephew was not renewed. Nothing daunted, he left Ireland and became the chief tax adviser to the dictator of Ghana where he prospered for many years.

14

> He had in the Court of King's Bench used rough language towards Mr Hackett, a gentleman of the Bar. The members of which profession considered themselves as all assailed in the person of a brother barrister.
>
> A general meeting was therefore called by the Father of the Bar. A severe condemnation of His Lordship concluded and voted with only one dissident voice. An unprecedented resolution was entered into 'that until His Lordship publicly apologised, no barrister would either take a brief, appear in the King's Bench or sign any pleading for that court'.
>
> The experiment was actually tried. The judges sat, no counsel appeared. There was no alternative and next day, the Lord Chancellor published a very ample apology by advertisement in the newspaper and with excellent address made it appear as if written on the evening of the offence and therefore voluntary.

That incident is recorded by Jonah Barrington and happened in the eighteenth century. It was 150 years later that the Irish Bar felt compelled to censure Judge Fawsett in a similar manner.

Tommy Doyle, then a spritely young barrister, was briefed in an appeal in the town of Naas in the spring of 1947. His client, a young army sergeant, had been convicted in the District Court of dangerous driving, and had been fined and sentenced to six months hard labour. Unfortunately someone had been seriously injured in the accident.

The case arose out of a collision between a hackney car and an army vehicle, and whatever the driving may have been like, to give a twenty-two year old married soldier six months hard labour for a road traffic offence was savage. Thinking he had a good case on the merits, as indeed he had, there not being much evidence of criminal driving, Tommy did not attempt to address the judge on the sentence as he felt he should win his appeal. Fawsett confirmed the conviction and in an irascible manner threw the papers down on top of the county registrar's head, snarling, 'Appeal dismissed.'

Coming out of court, Tommy Doyle found his client in tears. The man would now be cashiered from the army, he would have no job to support his newborn child and young wife, he was in absolute despair. If the prison sentence were removed and a fine substituted with the suspension of his licence, he would be retained in the army.

Tommy returned to court and, when the next case finished, stood up and said he wanted to mention the last appeal.

'This case is closed. I will not hear you.'

'There are several matters I would like to bring to your attention, m'Lord. You may remember, wrongfully thinking I had a good case, I did not address you on the sentence and the effect it will have on this young man and his prospects in the army and his future there.'

'Rarely have I listened to a worse case of dangerous driving, I should have increased the sentence', said Fawsett, 'I will not hear you.'

'I intend to be heard and to press the matter', said Doyle. 'This is vital for my client.'

'I told you to sit down.'

'I refuse to sit down, I must be heard. If your Lordship knew the full effects of this decision on my client, you would deal more leniently with him. I would suggest a suspension of his licence and a fine instead of imprisonment.'

'I do not want to hear you. I said the matter is closed, I told you to sit down. Do so at once.'

'But you must ....'

'Do you not understand the meaning of words? I said I do not want to hear you. The matter is absolutely closed. I was most lenient with your client, his was a disgraceful example of criminal recklessness.'

'He is going to lose his position. I must put these facts before you, he is married man with a small child. I am asking you to hear his evidence and remove or if you think fit, suspend the prison sentence.'

'I will not do so.'

'I insist that you hear me and my submission.'

'Sit down at once.'

Tommy Doyle said he would not sit down.

The judge shouted to the Garda in charge of the court: 'Guard, come forward, arrest that man', pointing to Doyle. No such words had ever been used to a member of the legal profession before.

Garda Muldoon, one of our favourite members of the force, with great reluctance advanced from the door of the court down to the well of the chamber and touched Tommy on the shoulder. The latter impatiently shook the hand off and marched out of court shouting.

'I protest in the strongest possible manner. You are not behaving in a way befitting the bench.'

'You have made your protest, sir, now leave or I will commit you to Mountjoy Prison for contempt.'

'I have not finished my protest.'

Tommy left the court accompanied by the Garda. He hastened back to Dublin, and in the early afternoon made a complaint to Henry Moloney, who promptly summonsed the Bar Council. For once they did something. As in Lord Clonmel's case, a resolution was passed and a letter was dispatched by hand the next day to the judge demanding an apology to Mr Thomas Doyle.

The resolution as passed stated that the Bar was of the opinion that Judge Fawsett was not entitled to order the arrest and removal from court of Mr T.A. Doyle, Barrister at Law, and that such arrest and removal constituted a serious infringement of the rights of counsel. It further went on to state that in the event of the judge's refusing to apologise for his action, members of the Bar should not practise in his court until such time as an adequate apology to Mr Doyle, in open court, was forthcoming.

There was no apology. The following Monday the Circuit Court sat at Trim. No barrister appeared. The first civil action was called and Captain Cowan, a very flamboyant solicitor in his time and no liker of Dermot Fawsett, said:

'Counsel refuses to accept a brief to appear before your Lordship and I therefore apply for an adjournment.'

The other solicitors all stated that they were in the same position and their briefs were out, but no counsel appeared. The boycott was absolute and every case was adjourned. Matters became serious and of public concern when criminal trials were postponed. Some of the younger barristers were not completely in favour of the strike, they could not see its resolution — no fees were coming in.

Privately it was said that Judge Fawsett would never apologise. He was quoted as saying that he could only be removed by a resolution of both Houses of Parliament, until someone pointed out to him that as far as he was concerned, this was not the case. The office of a Circuit Court Judge is not one established by the Constitution and has not got the immunity and protection given to the High Court by the Constitution.

At last the Bar Council was informed that an apology would be made at Trim Circuit Court. There was a large attendance on that day. Many people had applications of an urgent nature and there was a long list.

The judge came out on the bench. He sat with dignity and, looking down, stated that he was delighted to see Mr Thomas Doyle in court, who had come there by his invitation.

To the room, packed with barristers, journalists and solicitors and gapers of all sorts, he said that six weeks ago he had felt himself obliged, for the preservation of order in his court, to request Mr Doyle's removal by a Garda Sergeant. Mr Doyle wanted a case reheard. He then said that at the time the application by Mr Doyle was made, he had proceeded on to a Workmen's Compensation Act case which had not been disposed of.

'I told Mr Doyle,' he said 'that I had finally disposed of the Criminal Appeals and that I could not hear him, but Counsel relied on his right of audience and persisted in addressing the court. As judge, I asked him to desist and sit down. I was disobeyed. Ultimately, I ordered him to be removed by the Garda Sergeant and he was removed.

'I now say, Mr Doyle, I have asked you here that I might tell you publicly that I regret I am sorry for the order. At the time you addressed me and insisted upon being heard, I had not averted to the real grounds of your application, namely that I had refused to hear you as counsel in the Criminal Appeal that morning. It was the ground on which you asked me to hear in the afternoon, although I had endeavoured to recall what happened in the early morning, I had failed to do so because apparently nothing unusual transpired during the hearing of the Criminal Appeal and nothing unusual transpired afterwards. I have no recollection that you asked me to rehear your case and that I cast you aside. If that were true then I must admit that I made a mistake. Accordingly I express my regret and sorrow that I ordered you to leave the court.'

There was no admission by the learned judge that he had had

Tommy Doyle arrested in court, nor apology for it.

Doyle got up and made suitable mumblings and said he would be glad to refer to the happy relations which existed between the judge as presiding judge on the one hand and himself as a member of the Bar, glad to think these happy relations would continue. Thereupon we all thought the incident was closed and badly closed at that.

Fawsett, however, went on to say that he wished, as judge, to address the particular practitioners on a Circuit relating to the relations between the bench and the Bar. The view had been expressed recently, he said, that a judge was not entitled in any circumstances to order the arrest of a barrister and that to do so constituted a serious infringement of the rights of counsel. That, in his opinion, was unsound in law and he thought it was right that practitioners on a Circuit should know his understanding of the law on the subject. Barristers, he said, had many rights and privileges, immunity from arrest was not the right of any barrister, it is a privilege. He said that where a judge thought a barrister was guilty of contempt, it was proper to attach him and have him arrested, or if he was guilty of disorderly conduct the judge might order his removal from the court. He went on to say that he would do this whenever he thought fit.

This gives some idea of the atmosphere which prevailed in that court for over fifteen years. Many thought that the strike should have continued.

15

As years passed Judge Fawsett, very much mellowed, and growing into a kindly man of three score and ten, he retired. His successor, Kenneth Deale, with his tall wavy figure and benevolent friendly air, was a great contrast to Dermot. He started life in the claims department of the Zürich Insurance Company, did the Bar exams, studied in the evenings and was called. Leaving the company and quickly in good practice, his rapid advance made him unpopular with the insurance barristers who never lost the opportunity to denigrate him. I never found any of the criticisms of Kenneth justified. He fought his cases well and fairly and was a gentleman.

He proved to have a very broad range of interests, had great tolerance, professed to be an atheist, was extremely interested in law and after many years of service in the Circuit Court was transferred to the High Court, but unfortunately died soon afterwards. He would have made a great contribution to liberal legal development in this country.

As a judge he was most even-tempered and patient, everybody felt at their ease and happiness was restored to the halls and foyers of the court. He remembered that people giving testimony do so probably for the first time in their lives and indeed may never have been inside the precincts of a courtroom; much latitude should be given to such people and this they received. By cool effective questions, it is just as easy to detect a liar as by abrupt and bullying tactics. Instances of deliberate falsehood are rare. If a man is determined to lie, the administration of the oath will make no difference, invariably he will be caught out. Although he was meticulous in the observance of the rules of court, insisting on everything being correct in notices, motions and affidavits and trying all cases strictly in accordance with the Rules of Evidence, Judge Deale did not adopt that attitude to be obstructive. He believed in deciding a case according to the law. However harsh a decision might be, if it was in conformity with legal principles, the legal action succeeded.

All barristers practising before him became experts in the Law of Evidence and we constantly kept either Phibson or Cross, both textbooks on that topic, under the desk to ensure that the testimony adduced was admissible.

On Kenneth's first visit to Wexford, after he had dined, there was a knock on the door. He was informed that a senior garda officer was waiting. Thinking it was a courtesy call, he welcomed him in and invited him to have a drink. He was perfectly astonished, however, when he was handed a list of statistics of crime in the neighbourhood and a synopsis of the characters of those to be tried. He received no more visitors like that.

Brian Price gave me one of my first cases before the new judge. A lady had been convicted in the District Court of selling drink and keeping open her public house for hours after closing time on a Sunday evening. She lost her licence and appealed to the Circuit Court. The real culprit, however, was her husband, who was known as 'The Duke Murphy'. Arriving at the courthouse, I was astonished to see that in a corner of the hallway of the Naas building, there was a very fine three-piece drawing-room suite, consisting of two armchairs and a large couch, all in real leather.

There sat a lady of indeterminate age, wearing a fur coat from some indeterminate animal. 'The Duke', her husband, was many years younger.

'Aveatque Vale', said Mr Duke Murphy, taking me by the hand. This, I remember, was the name of a racehorse. He spoke a sort of jargon, a race-goers' rhyming slang.

I began to explain to Mrs Murphy the seriousness of her position, endeavouring to get some coherence out of her. Perhaps a mitigating explanation as to her conduct. Eventually the Duke became impatient.

'Baby honey,' said he, 'Charley Weld, Charley Weld. Listen in, Listen in.' Mr Weld was a well-known trainer who was the owner of a very popular racehorse called Listen In.

On the case being called, the prosecutor outlined the facts. The sergeant then came up and gave his evidence very slowly. Deale was not a quick judge and he liked to make a note of everything.

'Five minutes before midnight on the Sunday, closing time being ten o'clock,' said the sergeant, 'I knocked at the door of the defendant's public house. One of my men was around the back, where the gate was located. They could not stop the escape of some twenty or so persons, who charged over the rear wall.'

'Eventually we effected an entrance. A junior barman opened

the door.'
'Well, tell the judge what was the position then?'
'Before going in, we heard a lot of music, shouting, singing and laughter.'
'Yes.'
'On gaining entrance we saw Mrs Murphy at the piano, playing and singing.'
Deale, who fancied himself as a singer and a player of the piano, asked what was the song.
'I think it was something about a bull in a bush; she continued playing.'
'Mr Murphy was behind the counter upon which stood tumblers and pints of stout, some unfinished and some half finished, and glasses of whiskey.'
'I said to Mr Murphy, "Do you know it is well past the time for closing?"'
'What was his reply?'
'He said, "aw, fuck off!"'
Kenneth's glasses went down to the end of his nose. He said, 'What?'
The sergeant repeated and watched the judge's pen. He wrote the epithet down.
'I then spoke to the licensee, Mrs Murphy. She wouldn't stop her song.
'When she finished she gave a right thump of the piano and shouted to her friends, directing her voice towards the members of the Gardaí.
'She shouted, "Look at them, the shower of c--ts."'
Deale looked at him with astonishment and wrote it down. At this stage things, I may say, were looking very bad for the survival of the Murphys' licence.
'What can you say about this, Mr MacKenzie?'
I pointed out to the judge that a wife who commits an offence or crime of any sort when under the dominion of her husband, is presumed to be so influenced by him as not to have a criminal mind. Compulsion forced this lady to act in the way she did. Married to a much younger husband, a bullying type, whom it was known frequently threatened violence if not actually perpetrated this upon her, what could she do? I quoted authorities.
'She had no will of her own and was not the possessor of a

guilty mind, an essential factor in every crime.'

Kenneth became bemused and forgot all about the appalling language which he had heard. He became immersed in a novel point of law. The books changed the case. He gave her the benefit of the doubt, as to whether she had the *mens rea*, as the criminally disposed mind is called in law, and allowed the appeal.

It was a triumph, but in vain. The beautiful couch upon which we had sat during the consultation had been seized by the sheriff: it was the property of the Duke and his wife. Shortly after, the pub was sold. The Duke and his Duchess disappeared.

Prosecutors always had an easy run with most Circuit Judges, who firmly believed the man in the dock was guilty and, as far as they could within the limits of the law, wished to see him convicted and punished. With Kenneth Deale it was different. The general public may wonder how barristers defend ruffians and villains. It is a game. Counsel getting an acquittal for a prisoner receives from his colleagues unreserved congratulations on his victory. Usually, not only had the victor to convince the jury, but he had to fight a second adversary, in the person of the judge. The judiciary in the Circuit Court backed up the prosecutors. All this changed when Kenneth arrived. The whole onus was placed on the State, and the defence got every consideration and latitude.

At this time, I began to do a fair criminal business. The accused men, there being no legal aid in those days, usually produced £50 which was split between my solicitor and myself. No case lasted more than a day. But the trial was as hard fought and as skilfully done as if it had taken a week, the period occupied by most legally aided trials now.

If no points were taken or an objection made to any evidence, Kenneth immediately called upon the prosecuting counsel to justify it and required from him legal authority, if necessary. The submissions had to be made by the prosecutor and the legal situation explained for the assistance of the judge. The defence literally had nothing to do but sit back, nobody pleaded guilty any more. It was better to take your chance.

Pleading guilty is a risky enough business in our country. There is no such thing as the American plea bargaining. I attempted this on only one occasion.

Through a temporary illness of Kenneth, we had a judge from

LAWFUL OCCASIONS

Dublin during his absence. I had been briefed to defend an up and coming jockey then riding in Ireland.

It was the usual sexual offence, committed against a willing girl, who was under the age of seventeen. In cases, it's no defence to say that she was experienced and consented, or that she looked twenty-one. The age constitutes the crime. My client had made a statement admitting the offence. The act was committed outside a dance hall in Newbridge. The girl was extremely willing, for she had already been with two men before she induced the jockey to try a mount.

The Barrow shimmered and the sun shone on the Athy courthouse, it was a beautiful summer's day in July. The Galway races were taking place that evening, commencing at six o'clock. My client was engaged to ride in one of the flat feature races.

Before the case was due to start, Cyril Maguire, who was the prosecutor, and I went into the chamber of the strange judge. I suggested that if I pleaded guilty, perhaps he would impose a suspended sentence. I was not received in too friendly a way. His Lordship sniffed and hissed and walked up and down the room saying, 'This is a most serious offence', and sucking his breath in between his teeth.

'The only reason I'm taking this unusual course,' I said, 'is that if he goes to prison, no matter what the offence is, that's the end of his career. His jockey's licence is gone, then he's lost his employment, and he's a very good character.'

There was more sucking and hissing.

'He's only twenty-two years of age and he's never had any trouble before and it is no disrespect to the young lady to say that the girl was extremely mature.'

'I couldn't possibly do a thing like that, I certainly couldn't.' The learned judge paced up and down hissing and sucking. 'There's far too much of this in these country parts. An example must be made. Young men will have to learn that they cannot seduce and corrupt girls of that age. I can't possibly accede to your request.'

'Very well', I said and I left the room.

Cyril had made a sympathetic clucking noise in my support.

'I'll fight it anyway', said I. 'It's the most hopeless case I've ever had, but I'll have a go at it.'

The statement made to the Gardaí had, my client claimed,

109

been improperly induced.

The Gardaí, of course, denied this, remarking that spontaneously when charged he made the statement and that they had warned and cautioned him that he need not say anything, but if he did, it would be taken down in writing and used in evidence.

The prosecutrix was a very bad witness. I managed to confuse the poor girl as to where and when she had been with my client. She got hopelessly mixed up, admitting she was with other men that night saying only that they were all a right lot of 'go-boys'.

After a short absence, the jury acquitted my client. The accused did not give evidence.

It was four in the afternoon. He would easily make the races. His ride was at seven o'clock. Having thanked my solicitor and myself and having paid his £50 he emerged from the court to shake hands with the jury.

'Have you a tip for us?' said one of them.

'Back me tonight in the seven o'clock race, I'm a certainty. My horse is a flyer and is carrying no weight.'

Facing the waters of the river Barrow, near the bridge and about 200 yards from the courthouse was a bookmaker's office. He traded under the name of Hugh Lupus. Like the start of a marathon race, the jury charged as one man to get their money on. Every penny in their pockets was laid in Mr Lupus' office on the tip from the jockey's mouth.

My client finished down the field. I had always been warned never to take a jockey's tip.

In my career I only prosecuted two cases. Two barmen had ingeniously falsified the books and records of a Bord na Móna canteen and had made off with a large quantity of stock. This was my first prosecuting case. Had they been managers of banks or big companies, they would have been respected millionaires. I had a miserable weekend trying to sort out the evidence. Dermot Fawsett was the judge in that case but I don't believe he understood it any more than I did.

The second case involved a row one New Year's Eve in the town of Kilcock. Two young men were involved. One struck the other a blow, knocking him to the ground. The local doctor was summoned, an extremely gentlemanly person, who looked at the injured man, decided that his problem was drink and told his companions to bring him home to bed. Unfortunately, his skull was fractured, and he died the next day from a brain haemorrhage.

Joe Lynch was for the defence. He was the most taciturn man at the Bar. He lived in the University Club and I called for him and drove him down to court every day. He never spoke during the journeys.

At the end of the second day it was decided to sit late and finish the case. The jury were sent off at four o'clock for tea, biscuits and slop. The judge said that they could consider the case during the interval and if they decided to acquit the accused, they might do so, but if not they would have to hear the summing up and charge from him.

Unfortunately, when we came back after the interval, Joe never asked had the jury made a decision, something he could have found out from the usher. They had indeed decided to acquit the man, but after two hours of the judge's charge, they changed their view and convicted. He was sentenced to one year imprisonment, subsequently quashed by the Court of Criminal Appeal.

16

Never having been to the west of Ireland until the High Court began to sit in Galway, I was quite amazed at the colourful scene on that Circuit. The pace of life there was extremely rapid.

A number of barristers were devoted to fishing, both Chris Micks and Oliver Gogarty being outstanding in this field. Every August Chris went to fish in Scotland accompanied by his sister and an elderly lady who was a neighbour of mine when I lived in Killiney. One year, towards the end of the month, he caught five salmon. A Polaroid picture was taken of a beaming Chris standing for this almighty catch. Placing the photograph in an envelope with a card, he wrote to Bill Finlay with the words 'nunc dimitius'. Two hours later he died.

Suffering a lot from arthritis, the pain was an excuse for his numerous Gordon's and tonic. He maintained a great style for the Circuit appeals in Castlebar, he brought down the butler from the King's Inns, who every day in that primitive courthouse, served on a gleaming white tablecloth, with good silver and glassware, lobsters and salmon for lunch. The butler also supervised the dining room in Pelly's Hotel where the head waiter had recently departed. This man had come to Castlebar as a bookmaker, setting up business shortly before the Grand National, which was won by the Irish horse, 'Workman'. He closed the shop the next day, went to the hotel and obtained the job.

On one occasion, Chris came down in his dressing gown and said to the butler, 'Lane, what about my breakfast now?' At which Lane pointed out to him that it was seven o'clock in the evening and dinner would shortly be ready.

His disposition could be refractory at times. A young junior attempted to prevent him from driving his car when he was in no condition to do so. Chris, refusing to hand over the keys, belaboured the young man with his walking stick.

One of the old members of that Circuit was Mick Carson. He practised mainly in the Land Commission which, before constitutional actions were taken against it, was the most unholy, bureaucratic body of tyrants. When their activities were challenged in the courts, Mick Carson had to stand over them. When confronted not only by unconstitutional conduct and legal argument, to which there was no answer, he would look earnestly at the Supreme Court and observe:

'You ask for my answer, all I can say is this, the Land Commission are as decent a body of men as you can find anywhere in the world.'

Tommy Connolly, our greatest constitutional lawyer, also started his career in the Western Circuit and occasionally came for the jury actions, but these cases were not exactly his cup of tea. Held in March, they usually coincided with the Cheltenham race meeting. Tommy had very few briefs on his last visit to Galway, but he cleaned out two bookmakers. He seldom attended a race meeting, but was a student of form, and had often brought off the autumn double.

Rathmullen House is a charming place on the shores of Lough Swilly. The judges stay there when on Circuit. Kindly ladies bring in country house breakfasts of porridge and cream, bacon, eggs, sausages and tomatoes. Beside the log fire after dinner, Bobby Barr, who was my colleague on the occasion, held up his index finger and showed me a scar.

'I'll tell you how I got this', he said.

A constitutional action had come Bobby's way. At this stage, Tommy Connolly, almost in his eighties, was briefed to appear with him. In addition to being an admittedly heavy drinker, Tommy was never without a cigarette dangling from his lips, enveloping his not very well pressed suit in a snow storm of ashes. So absent-minded was he, that I have seen him with his pyjamas still under his trousers. The boys would carry the books into court and Tommy would launch into his argument. The dry law, moistened by classical allusions, left members of the Supreme Court flapping with the honey of his legal arguments.

During the long vacation, Bobby had arranged to visit his leader at his home in Northumberland Road. On opening the door, Mrs Connolly regretfully said that Tommy had not yet come home, but as Bobby was expected would he please come in and wait. The house was an extensive Victorian building with a large drawing-room. The astonished Bobby saw that the floor was covered with layer upon layer of newspaper. He soon realised why. On a tall perch, uncaged, was a large parrot hopping from foot to foot, glaring malevolently at him. The reason for the newspapers was then apparent as the bird flew freely around the room, landing anywhere it wished.

Presently, all apologies, Tommy arrived, sat down at a table, also newspapered. Spattering the legal documents with ash, he rummaged through them. With a flurry of wings, the parrot hovered in the air and eventually settled down on his master's head. There he perched all through the deliberations and scrutiny of the documents, his beady eyes glaring at Bobby. When the business was over, the parrot perched on Tommy's arm, opened his beak wide and shot out his tongue, a long narrow object. His master made some birdlike twitters.

'He loves this, watch!'

Tommy enthusiastically started to rub the tongue with his forefinger. The bird, making orgiastic coos, hopped more excitedly from one leg to the other.

'I believe he likes you too, Bobby.'

'Oh, I don't think so.'

'I can tell by the way he's looking at you.'

Tommy gave the tongue more strokes.

'Here, Bob, you try it.'

Not wishing to be impolite, Bobby gingerly placed his forefinger on the tongue. Like a lobster's claw, the beak snapped.

'And that's how I got this scar on my finger', said Bobby.

The later personality in the west, though no less forceful, was Paddy Lindsay, scholar, politician and Senior Counsel. I once described him to a jury as having the style of an eighteenth century gentleman, which pleased him greatly. This counteracted his ploy before a Galway jury of telling them that he appeared for the plaintiff, while his good friend *from Dublin*, Mr MacKenzie, appeared for the defendant. This xenophobic approach shouldn't have worked, but it did.

He defended a client in Castlebar before a jury. The prosecution's case was weak. Paddy, full of self confidence, assured of an acquittal, urged the jury in emotional tones:

'Gentlemen, you do not need to hear my speech in this case to convince you of my client's innocence. You heard the evidence against him, not a tittle tattle of proof is there in this case. I won't weary you, I merely ask you to acquit him.'

Expecting a verdict in a short time, he went across the road to Pelly's and ordered a cup of tea. An hour passed, no jury, two hours and then three. He was in agony. Had he made one of the greatest mistakes of his life in not pounding home to twelve good men and true the many points in favour of his client's innocence? They couldn't be so dense as not to follow all the points in cross-examination.

The usher came over.

'The jury is ready now for Lindsay.'

Trembling, he crossed the road into the courthouse, the ancient primitive building I have described, but which I would not see changed for anything.

Perched up high in the jury box were the solemn-faced twelve. In came the judge, the paper was handed in — not guilty.

'The verdict of you all?'

Paddy nearly fainted with relief and rushed over to the hotel to get himself a large libation. In dribs and drabs the jurists came in after the long ordeal to slake their thirst. Paddy, also a well known politician, shook them all by the hand, saying, 'Thank you, gentlemen, that was a good job done.'

They all nodded and attacked their pints. Eventually he said:

'In the name of Jasus what took you so long about the case, sure the man was so obviously innocent, how could it have presented any problem?'

The man who had been the foreman laughed:

'It presented no problem', he said. 'We made up our minds and decided the case in ten minutes. But sure there are many of us old friends and we hadn't met some of us for twenty-five years.'

Liam Collins, a popular and efficient manager of the claims department of an insurance company, frequently visited Galway on business. Paddy, hearing that he had become engaged to be married, was all curious.

'This is good news I hear about you, Liam.'

'Why, thank you.'

'Getting married is a good idea, even though you may be a bit later than most of us, I expect you will be very happy. Now tell me, where does the girl come from?'

'She comes from Tipperary.'

'Aw indeed, a great county, very rich land, a lovely place.'

'Yes that's right.'

'And is there a farm?'

'Yes, there is.'

'About how many acres now?'

'250 I think.'

'Oh, that's grand, really grand. You're very lucky then, I congratulate you. Tell me how many are in the family?'

'There's eight brothers and sisters.'

Paddy's face clouded a bit. 'How many girls? ... And where does she come in the family?'

'She's the second last girl.'

With a sorrowful gaze at him, Paddy said, 'Liam, I'll tell you this, you'll be lucky to get the fresh eggs at Christmas.'

Naturally Paddy lived in Dublin. On a school run to Mount Anville convent early one morning, his car stalled at Goatstown at the traffic lights close to the well-known restaurant. The exasperated drivers behind could not understand firstly why Paddy could not move on, and secondly why, if his engine were defunct, he did not get out of his car and have a look.

The reason was he was still in his pyjamas.

The Circuit was dominated also by John Willie O'Connor, an old schoolfellow of mine, who never took silk, although he had a most extensive practice.

Never taking a drink until thirty-five years of age, he made up for lost time. A bachelor, it was his custom every night to dine in the Dolphin and fall asleep with his head on the table. His dining companions were non-stop talkers. Although John Willie was recumbent, they continued conversing as if he were in rapt attention. Eventually the waiters would come and lift him up in a most kindly manner and put him into a taxi. Later when he was made a judge, he caused quite a sensation when he was alleged to have fallen asleep during the trial of four people accused of taking part in the Sallins train robbery. John maintained that although his eyes were closed he heard everything.

He was in Blackrock College in my time and was called to the Bar a year earlier than I was. Gambling was his great passion. He worked hard throughout his first year travelling on Circuit, and made some money which he promptly lost at the Phoenix Park 1500 race meeting in August.

116

He had a strong antipathy to the sort of Gaels who paint out English signposts and who have that mentality which refused to allow the Galway soccer team to use the GAA ground in the city for the only important soccer match they ever managed to arrange. Besieged in the bar in the Imperial Hotel by some of these people who were attacking him for his lack of patriotism and his indifference to things Gaelic, he turned to a neighbour and said, 'I want to get rid of these *amadáns*. Can you tell me the Irish word for "off"? I know the other.'

It is customary to give a dinner for the judges who are assigned to try the cases in Galway. The Bar are the hosts. These are formal black tie affairs.

On one very well attended occasion, not surprisingly, John Willie fell asleep, this time before the dinner. (Thereafter a practice was introduced by Oliver Gogarty and Tom Hannon, that speeches were to be made early in the dinner. Firstly, soup was to be provided and then the speeches were to be made. Everyone could then merrily proceed to enjoy themselves.) The waitress came and placed a plate of soup in front of the recumbent guest, removed same, then placed the fish and the joint; all were untouched. One of the highlights of the evening was a magnificent baked Alaska which was brought in with great pride by the chef, who displayed it before putting it on the table. The flames and the heat must have affected John, for he suddenly woke up, roared and stretched himself, took out his false teeth and threw them plonk into the middle of the pudding.

A number of people practise all over the west without ever coming to Dublin except on occasions. In the early days after 1922, a K.C. called Fitzgerald Kenny had a considerable practice. Potential clients used to arrive in droves up to his large country house in Mayo, where he greeted them at the hall door. They were not asked in. He would listen to them and say, 'You have an unanswerable case, go immediately to your solicitor.'

Five minutes later, perhaps, one of the parties on the other side would arrive to receive exactly the same advice.

Roars and shouts were relied upon by many old time advocates rather than the subtlety of questions which led the witness into a trap. Fitz defended a young man who was charged with having carnal knowledge of a girl under age. The case seemed

117

absolutely hopeless. There was an eyewitness, a rare event to such an occurrence. A farm labourer who had been slashing a hedge, saw the performance taking place in a field close to where he was working. He gave evidence of this. He had seen it all.

Fitz stood up with a glare on his face, fixed an angry eye on him and shouted:

'Aren't you the dirty auld divil!'

His man was acquitted.

Fitz had a noticeable lisp, just as Chris Micks had. They were on different sides in a case one day which concerned an assault, and they had drawn a strange judge.

Fitz opened his case, referring to the 'wow' that had broken out in a certain public house. The judge looked puzzled.

'A wow, Mr Fitzgerald Kenny?'

'Yes m'Lord, a really bad wow.'

'What exactly do you mean?'

Then Chris spoke up:

'He means m'Lord, a wow, in other words a wumpus.'

The gentlemen of Galway are the proud possessors of a County Club, which used to be housed in the Square. It is managed and run by two excellent ladies, sisters, Rosie and Gertie. I first visited the club on the invitation of Chris Micks to lunch.

We went to the dining room in which all the members sat at one long table. It was heaped with rolls and brown bread and many jugs of milk. The fare was wonderful homemade soup, always roast meat or roast chicken, with huge quantities of steaming potatoes, cooked in their jackets, cabbage or carrots. Then there was rice pudding or tapioca, followed by tea or real coffee. The cost was ridiculously small. The club was eventually bought out by an insurance company but moved to a new premises at the Weir in Galway, where the same tradition was carried on.

I often remarked to these ladies that they were responsible for the Pope's visit to Galway. They had gone to Rome several times. The dispensation lifting the restriction of meat eating on Fridays for Catholics was ignored by them for many years, fish or omelettes only being served on that day in the club. They still continue to welcome the members in the warmest fashion and still steadfastly refuse even to contemplate the presence of a lady in that last bastion of Clubland.

118

17

Like Bertie Wooster, and other P.G. Wodehouse characters, many of my friends, and I myself, had eccentric aunts. Into this category fell my mother's sisters, of whom I was extremely fond. Raymond Hickey, who went through college with me but became a solicitor, went into Arthur Cox's offices as a young man. He was a very brilliant humorous fellow who died very prematurely. He had an aunt, well into her eighties, who lived in an old Victorian house in Aughrim Street. I have no doubt that he contributed to her support, though she was fearfully independent. One Sunday afternoon he called out to visit her. He found her in floods of tears. She handed him a notice — from the Dublin Corporation. It was a menacing document, informing her that unless she repaired the sewer pipe leading from her premises and connected to the public roadway — the point where it had become damaged being the junction of the main sewer — she would be liable to a fine of £500. The milkman, she sobbed, had told her that to do this job would be 'terrible dear', and she had no money. What was she to do?

And indeed it was a dear job. Work would entail opening up her front garden, going through the concrete of her path, out onto the roadway, right across to the sewer which was on the far side. It would involve possibly a watchman. A figure of £250 had been put on this which was a very large sum in those days.

Raymond tried to soothe her, but she kept on sobbing. It amounted to half her year's income. She'd have no money for the rent, the future was absolutely black. To give some inkling of what £500 represented at that time, Raymond had, in a good job, £4.10s per week with Arthur Cox & Co.

Mr Cox's office was one of the best in the city and did an enormous business. Plenty of contacts could be made through its clients. Raymond would see what he could do.

He didn't achieve very much. Workmen from the Corporation came out to his aunt to know when was the work going to start. They'd have to do it themselves and charge her. Otherwise take her to court. The tears and lamentations continued.

There being nothing to be done among the clients in the office,

Raymond went down to the Corporation. He contacted the lowliest solicitor there and eventually, after about a fortnight's extremely hard lobbying, was introduced to the man who really mattered, who said he would look into it and could Raymond call him again in a week.

Seven days later back trundled poor Raymond to the Corporation office. In the circumstances, yes, they'd do something for the lady. They had examined the situation, discovering that the old sewerage scheme was breaking down and they would have to replace it all in a few months time. She needn't bother doing anything. Raymond thanked him and went immediately to Aughrim Street. As she opened the door, he shouted to the aunt:

'It's all right, it's all right, everything is fixed.'

'What are you talking about?'

'The drain, the sewer, nothing to worry about, it's all fixed, they'll mend it, you won't have to pay anything.' He was surprised at the aunt's complacency. She merely nodded.

'Well,' he said in astonishment, 'what do you say, what do you think?'

'I knew it all along.'

Raymond stared at her.

'Yes, I knew it all along.'

'You knew it all along?'

'Last week,' said she, 'last week I knew what the only thing to do was and I did it.'

'What was that?'

'I put a miraculous medal into the toilet, and flushed it down the drain.'

Each March and June in the Law Library sweeps were held on the Grand National and Derby. These events were organised by the youngest juniors, presumably because they had time to do this. Invariably, to everyone's annoyance, the sweeps were won by those with the greatest practice. It was customary to bring the organisers out and stand them a really good lunch.

Many of us were extremely interested in racing. Some were racehorse owners. Frank Roe is the doyen of the racing members of the Bar, now a steward of the Turf Club, owner and marvellous amateur rider. He could still ride in an amateur race, though he has just retired from the bench and he was never shy about telling people when to back him. Early in the 1950s he was riding one of his own horses in Punchestown.

A large party of us organised a jaunt to Punchestown, complete with picnic baskets, champagne, smoked salmon and all the delicacies of a race track lunch alfresco. Opening at about six to one, the odds shortened on Frank down to about threes. All our money was on him. It was a three mile steeplechase and Frank, well off at the start, appeared to be making good headway, but tailed a bit as they came down past the stand to start the second round of the course.

It was not until they came to about the third last that Frank really moved forward, making a great effort, riding with arms and legs. I don't think, however, he ever hit the horse. He was just beaten. He came over the last neck and neck with the ultimate winner, but his horse, obviously tired, failed to hold the course and drifted very far to the side and finished second.

Two days later, Frank came out again, same horse, and won a similar race at twenty-five to one. He explained to me afterwards:

'I could easily have won on Tuesday had I had a practice-run over the course. It was strange to me and I didn't really know it. The experience counted and that's how I won today; and I'll tell you, Paddy, I haven't had an effin' shilling on it.'

In the old days it was an unwritten rule, and I'm speaking before my time, that no cases would go on during the Punchestown meeting. Everything had to be disposed of or settled before 12.30 to allow the judges and everyone away. During the War supporters travelled by horse-drawn cabs, bicycles, even went by train to Naas, before petrol was restored.

The Bar was highly thrilled when Frank succeeded Kenneth Deale. He proved to be one of the best Circuit Court Judges that ever sat in Ireland, and afterwards became President of the Circuit Court. He just heard cases, apart from horses and racing he had no other interest in life. Sometimes he sat until late at night to dispose of actions. Everyone was made at ease before him and he ran an extremely happy, sensible court of justice.

One day Harry Hill had a fairly important brief in the county of Meath where Frank was sitting. Being anxious about time, he belted along the road as hard as he could drive and eventually arrived at Kells. There was no sign of life. The door of the court was locked. He waited around until the District Court clerk came from his office nearby.

'Ah sure,' said that worthy, 'you've come to the wrong place. Judge Roe is sitting in Trim today. The court is not on here till next week.'

'How long will it take me to get to Trim?'

'A good half hour or more.'

'Oh God,' said Harry, 'and I'm first on the list.'

'Come in and use the telephone.'

Harry dialled Trim Courthouse. As was to be expected, Frank answered, the only line being switched through to his room. Harry explained his predicament to Frank.

'I see,' said the judge, 'obviously you're not going to get here in time for this case. Who's your opponent?'

'Barry White', said Harry.

'Very well. Hold on a minute, Harry, and I'll see what I can do.' Barry White is also a great racing man, though not, I think, an amateur rider.

A few minutes elapsed, Frank came back to the phone and said, 'Are you still there, Harry?'

'Yes.'

'Barry's here with me now. What's the nature of your case?'

'It's a claim on foot of a contract for the hire of a bulldozer. My client has not been paid.'

'How much are you claiming, Harry?'

'£5,000.'

Harry could hear Frank talking to Barry:

'Barry, Harry says that he's claiming £5,000 against you for the hire of a bulldozer. How much are you going to give him?'

He also heard the reply:

'My client is complaining that the bulldozer was a bit bashed up before it came to him. It took three weeks to do the work which should have been finished in five days.'

'Ah, come on now,' said Frank, 'what are you going to give him?'

There was a pause. Frank came back to the phone.

'Harry, Barry says he'll give you £3,500 and no more, plus £500 for costs. What do you say?'

'Well, my fellow will accept it provided the money is paid within a month.'

The matter was disposed of.

While I'm on judges with Christian names of Frank, Judge Martin told me that when he was sitting on the Special Criminal Court he had an armed bodyguard. Frank's generosity and consideration for those who were burdened with such a job was such that they received from the judge many beakers of his favourite libation, brandy and ginger ale.

Some very good German friends of Frank, to whom he was indebted for kindness shown to one of his children, were invited by him to Ireland. After putting them up in his home in Kinsealy where he was neighbour to the Taoiseach, Frank drove them down to Ashford Castle for a weekend. Naturally the armed body guard attended. On the first day after exploring the grounds and the lake, a very good dinner was enjoyed by the German gentleman and his wife with Frank. The dinner being concluded, coffee taken into the lounge, Frank invited them into the bar for a liqueur before going to bed.

Who was in there but the bodyguard, in a very delicate condition, holding himself steady on the brass rail and looking benevolently over at his mentor and his guests. Goodnights were being said. Frank had arisen to shake hands with his guests when the minder staggered over.

'Now may I ask a question? Will yous have a drink now before yous go to bed?'

'Thank you very much, sir, but no.'

'Ah come on, you will, just one for the road.'

'Herr Judge Martin, my wife and I are very tired. We have enjoyed our day, but it was long and we would like to retire.' He turned to the guard. 'Thank you very much indeed for the invitation.'

'Yous will have to have one before you go, I insist.'

'No thank you, not at all.'

'Ah come on now, 'twill do you good.'

'Thank you, we are going.'

The bodyguard then assumed a thick German accent, leered at them and said, 'Come now. Ve haf vays of making you talk.'

Many people in the Library have owned or had shares in horses or have been in syndicates, but the spectacular owner was Desmond Bell. Called to the Bar a few years ahead of me, he quickly developed a fine practice, specialising in rent act cases. He had impressed Arthur Cox and had received a lot of work from that office, and his intuition had impressed Cecil Lavery so much that they were great friends and whenever he could, Cecil had him as his junior. I regarded his brain as being like lightning. He fastened on the real points in every complex case immediately.

He had great support among the intelligent solicitors who recognised his value and I did many cases with him.

On one occasion he had four actions going simultaneously in the Round Hall. This in the days of the small list. He conducted them like a non-playing captain. I was in one court, other colleagues dispersed in the other rooms. Des strolled in from time to time to see how everything was going, made suggestions, walked on to the next. They all turned out well.

Unfortunately, Des' horses always won when he didn't expect them even to be placed. Sam from the dressing room, as a holiday outing during the long vacation, went to an August meeting in the Curragh and invested a fiver with the tote on a horse of Des' which was running that day. There wasn't a shilling for it anywhere — and it romped home. Sam collected £300. A massive amount of money in those days.

The Library seethed with excitement one day when Des told us that a horse of his, running in Baldoyle, was an absolute certainty. Everyone was to go out and back it, which we all did. Some of us trooped out to Baldoyle to see the great event and a good party was promised afterwards.

At the races, in the ring, the trainer said to Des not to worry about going to the bookmakers to bet, that he had a runner who was getting the money on. Immediately before the off, Des was up in the Owners and Trainers, his hands shaking with excitement so much that he couldn't focus the race glasses properly.

'You got the money on?' he said to the trainer.

'Yes.'

'What price did you get?'

'Twelve to one.'

'But we're the favourite, the bookies are quoting 2/1 even 7/4.'

'I know, we're not on your horse, we're on to my outsider and it'll win.'

It did.

18

The Bar are great diners out. Hard work and play. Tension and anxiety produced by preparation and conduct of cases leads to a reaction.

In no profession can its members be so judged on their capabilities by lay people. Once a barrister is on his feet, the client knows whether he is good or bad. If he has performed poorly they usually say nothing. If he has done well they praise and they are grateful.

A good win or settlement deserved a lunch out. The sort of restaurants patronised by my colleagues were good old chop and steak houses, like the Dolphin and the Red Bank in the early days, the Oyster in Cork, the Tavern in Galway, which are now, with the exception of the Oyster, all gone. After the Dolphin closed, the great restaurant became the Lord Edward.

The waiters were and are marvellous. My friends and I usually tried to go to Frank's table. He was intensely interested in the law, the personalities in the profession, politics, economics and, above all, racing. Having seen me come up the hill (the expression used when approaching the restaurant!) with two people who shared with Frank political persuasions with which I did not actually agree, Frank once remarked 'I saw you on the road to Damascus.'

One afternoon, Ernest Wood, Peter McGuire, myself and others lunched well and long after a very good case and left rather late in the afternoon.

Two weeks later I was immersed in my study in the evening when the telephone rang. It was Frank.

'I have that little filly now', he said.

'What are you talking about, Frank?'

'That little filly, you remember we were talking about it. I have it now. I bought it.'

Recollection began to dawn on me.

'You remember you bought a half share, we're partners. I'll let you know how much the cheque is in a day or two.'

Horror, the recollection came back of agreeing to become a partner with Frank in the ownership of a two-year-old filly which he had spotted down in Tipperary.

'Keep your voice down, Frank', I said needlessly. I didn't want anyone in the household to know of my foolishness.

'It's unlikely, sir,' said Frank, 'that anyone can hear me.'

'All right,' I said, 'I'll be up to lunch tomorrow.'

And next morning I went to Eamon Walsh, who was recognised as the expert in the Law Library on horses. He was subsequently Master of the Galway Blazers.

'What am I going to do about this?' I asked him.

'First of all,' he said, 'do you have a cigarette, dear boy?'

'You know I don't smoke.'

'Pity.' Eamon didn't really approve of smoking. Although he would use a cigarette, he would never buy them. He made a great joke of this, as his minor eccentricity.

I told him the story of the filly.

'All you can do is this', he said. 'You have two options, run it for the season and lose a lot of money, or let it run once and see how it does — if badly, shoot it.'

I was rather gloomy about the whole thing. Frank told me it was going to run at a country meeting in the near future. I did not contact him about this.

I was on Circuit in the early spring, we had a very hard day down in Limerick. I went back to the small hotel where I usually stayed, the Woodfield, lay down on my bed and turned on the radio. The results were being given out of the four o'clock Maiden Fillies 2-Year-Old Race in Tralee — 1st: Gilded Lady, 2nd: Multo Vivace, which was the name of our horse.

I was bucked up considerably. I telephoned Frank who was ablaze with excitement.

'Next race is the Curragh', said he, 'in two weeks time. D'ya know what being second means? — We don't have to pay for transport to the races, so the next meeting the Racing Board do it for nothing.'

There was a big field at the Curragh for the next race; it was six furlongs, our filly broke away well, led most of the way and was pipped at the post by about a length by one of Vincent O'Brien's very expensive jobs.

And that was the saga of my solitary venture into racehorse ownership. She went to Mallow where she was certain to win, but the saddle slipped. At several country meetings she was beaten by

American-owned expensive animals, trained by Mr Dermot Weld, but was always placed.

Eventually, at the Rose of Tralee Festival in September, she won a good race and was retired for the season. The following year she was sold, I had had good year's sport, costing me nothing, and my capital was eventually returned intact.

I have written about the Dolphin, the Lord Edward and the Red Bank. Another wonderful restaurant seldom mentioned, except by English travel writers, is Chez Hans in Cashel. When Jim Carroll and Eddy Comyn were leading the Leinster Circuit, they decided to leave the frugal hotel in one of the Circuit towns and spend a couple of days in a more posh hotel. There the food was equally good. They were close to Chez Hans and could drive there some of the time. Bathed and shaved, they came down to the bar in the hotel and proceeded to select their drinks and food.

Jim thought that they should start with a bottle of champagne followed by a really good claret. The champagne presented no problems. Festus, the head waiter, who hailed from Ballinahinch in the west of Ireland and was a wonderful fisherman, stood there patiently while Jim scrutinised the wine list.

'How about the Bechevelle '67?'

'Oh! Very good, sir.'

'Is it ready for drinking?'

'I always have a few bottles of the good stuff like that ready. We have very discerning patrons here you know, sir, very prominent people with the horses.'

'The Montrose '67?'

'Excellent wine, sir.'

'And have you some out of the cellar?'

'Of course, sir, we always have.'

They consumed the champagne and just before the main course Jim sampled the Montrose. Now, I defy any person when he gets a small tablespoon full of wine in the bottom of a glass, unless the liquid stinks to high heaven, to determine whether it is of good quality or not. Jim passed it. It had a great body and a good aroma.

When full glasses were poured and they sipped the wine, they both expressed their disappointment to one another. They called the head waiter.

127

'Festus, this is not as good as we thought.'

'I'm very sorry, sir, I've looked after it myself. Would you like me to get you a bottle of something else?' He suggested something inferior.

They both agreed they would carry on with the wine they had although it was below their expectations.

About a year later they repeated the journey and spent the last two days of the Circuit week in the same posh hotel. They decided to order the exact same meal and sample another good claret. When they went down to the bar, they discovered that Festus wasn't there, it was his day off.

Perusing the wine list, Eddie decided that this time they would try the Bechevelle. The girl nodded and said that she would have to check that it was available.

A few moments later she came back.

'It's in the cellar, sir. Do you want me to do with it what Mr Festus does?'

They looked at her in some astonishment.

'I suppose you could open it now if you wished.'

'No, sir, not that, but will I do, sir, what Mr Festus...?'

'What does Mr Festus do?'

'He gets a bucket of boiling water and puts the wine in it for a few minutes.'

A great Dolphinite was Charlie Campbell, though not a luncher, it was usually on the way home that he went to the hostelry for a few balls of malt.

He was a tiny red-faced man with a subdued north of Ireland accent. He did a lot of work for Charlie Boyle who was an excellent trade union solicitor, specialising in claims brought against employers by workmen injured through neglect in the system of work or the unsafeness of the place of work.

Many of these cases were accidents while loading or unloading ships, and Charlie adopted a vernacular, which he thought was that of a stevedore and would appeal to the jury. He used to tell the jury that he was a sailor himself and had even voyaged around Cape Horn on a sailing ship as a lad.

I realised that there was something extraordinary about him when, in my very early days, I asked his opinion about a point of law.

'That's decided', he said 'in the House of Lords, in a case in which I was in. I'll get it for you.'

He went to the reports of appeal cases and returned with a House of Lords' decision and placed it on the desk.

'This reported case decided the question', said Charlie, pointing his finger. 'There I am.'

Impressed, I looked, then I said, 'But the name of the counsel is James Campbell, not Charles.'

'That's a mistake, a misprint, it was me.'

'You did a great job there, Charlie', I said.

'Yes, it's a pity they didn't put my name in rightly.'

James Campbell was a very successful Irish barrister who went to England and I believe was subsequently Lord Glenevy.

I soon learnt that a lot of amusement could be gained from a conversation with Charlie. He was always willing to give the benefit of his learning to a newcomer.

'Look, could you give me some help? I have a case about a jockey who fell during a steeplechase.'

'Ah yes, you've come to the right quarter.'

'I believe you one time used to ride in steeplechases.'

'Ride? Did I what? I rode in the Grand National on at least two occasions. I would have won once had my horse not been brought down by a faller.' Charlie couldn't ride a bicycle.

'Charlie, I've got this motor accident case and I'm sure you can help me. By the way, didn't you do some motor racing?'

'Did I what? I used to drive the old Bentleys in Brooklands. I raced also for Kay Donne's team in Le Mans. Magnificent cars they were. Now, let me see if I can get you a case on the point.'

There was indeed a case in which the Brooklands racing company were defendants. Again, Charlie produced it.

'I was in this case', he said.

Unfortunately no Campbell, or even a Charlie of any sort, was mentioned in the counsel who appeared. Nothing daunted, Charlie said, 'They forgot to put my name on the report, probably because it was shortly after the "Troubles", you know.'

For many years I plodded on as a junior, not taking silk until I had been twenty-eight years at the Bar. Practitioners become Senior Counsel much sooner nowadays, some after ten years practice. This I think is a pity. Many of them are grossly inexperienced and

CIE5005000

were it not for the tolerance of the present day judges, who are patient enough to listen to all sorts of rubbish, their poor examinations in chief and feeble cross-examinations, might bring them no business at all.

Other people with great junior practices were latecomers to the Inner Bar as well: Eamon Walsh, Frank Roe, Frank Martin. The trouble was that such juniors were imposed upon, doing the work that the seniors were supposed to do, yet getting less money. Although he had two Silks leading him, Frank was engaged by CIE specifically to cross-examine.

During these years I had a number of 'Devils'. The earliest were Maurice Gaffney and Ronan Keane. The former took silk years before I did and the latter is now a very eminent judge, author and fine legal brain.

Maurice is the most gentle of souls. He brings a philosophical and metaphysical element into every case. He was the only one to whom Seán Butler would listen with patience, never displaying irritation although Maurice would be the first person to admit that brevity was not one of his finer points.

Maurice and I were instructed by an insurance company to bring a claim against Aer Rianta, the managers and controllers of Dublin Airport.

A prominent Dublin surgeon had fulfilled his lifelong ambition of owning a really decent car. He purchased a gleaming red, two-seater, Mercedes Benz 500 sports car. Justifiably, he was inordinately proud of it.

Having to attend a medical conference in London which would take two days, he drove his car to the airport and left it in the general car park. This I think was in the days before there was long term parking. It was placed about fifty yards away from the admission barrier where there was a hut and still within sight of the people who should have been attending to the safety of their clients' vehicles. The key was in his possession, but unfortunately the ticket had been left in the glove compartment. A motor engineer had reported that for a thief to start the car without an ignition key would take approximately two hours work on the electrical system before the engine could be fired. Nevertheless, it was stolen.

The airport denied liability, pointing out that it was a

condition on their tickets, which of course was not brought to the surgeon's notice, that cars were parked at owners' risk, and they could not be responsible for the damage or theft. It became then a battle between the insurance company who recouped the surgeon, and the airport. How on earth we managed to get a jury in this case I don't know, but we did. The claim was laid in negligence as well as contract. All the case law and authorities were not on our side and we had to make new law. Maurice, on opening the case, had to explain to the jury what the contractual mind implied. He addressed the jury as follows:

'Gentlemen, I ask you now to put yourselves in the place of someone like my client, where you have come to a place of apparent safety, you have taken a ticket which obliges you to reimburse the airport for the custody of your car. In return, what do you expect from them? Surely it must be that your car will be safely supervised and safely returned to you. And is this not manifest by what would be your reaction and by the reaction of this eminent doctor when he returned and found his car was missing?

'If you were here in this situation would you not say, "Oh, heavens, my brand new expensive Mercedes Benz sports car is stolen"? If you said that, what would your next feeling be? Would you not say, "Oh dearie me, oh, dearie me, my lovely car has disappeared, my lovely car has been stolen"?'

Amongst my other devils, was former T.D. Dr John Kelly, who, had he wished, apart from being a brilliant scholar and an acute commentator, could have reached the top of the legal profession, had he continued in it.

Others were Simon O'Leary, now head of the Law Reform Commission; Frank Aylmer of the DPP's Department; Conal O'Toole, practising in Australia; Joe Matthews, in good practice here; Count Guy O'Kelly de Galway, a most eccentric Belgian and Irish country gentleman; and Eoghan Murnaghan, all doing good business.

19

After I had taken silk I found the work, although more remunerative, to be much less interesting and lacking a great deal of the human interest which I found so fascinating on Circuit. I was reluctant to take the step until practically dragged by Frank Griffin before the Chief Justice, who gave me a special call early in January 1972. I quickly got into quite a different type of practice and fortunately was employed by several insurance companies. My old solicitor friends on Circuit, however, stuck by me. But the hard slogging work at the desk at night evaporated, and the relief was like the disappearance of a toothache. I remained intensely interested nonetheless, in what went on in the Circuit.

My lunch consisted of a cup of coffee and a sandwich every day taken in the Four Courts Hotel. This old Georgian inn has now been demolished to make way for one of our hideous and ill-designed court office complexes.

Rex Mackey who was in practice in Donegal and Sligo before I came to the Bar, and who had left and worked in England for a while, returned to Ireland and shortly got into a good Circuit business. Rex is a great raconteur and mimic. At lunch time one day I asked him had he anything interesting coming up on the Circuit.

'There's a curious case which I have to do next week', he said. 'It's an appeal in Wicklow. Now you've had a lot of experience of strange cases in your life, well I'll tell you, you've never had the like of this before.

'I'm appearing for a fellow who's appealing against a month's imprisonment imposed upon him by a District Justice in Bray. He was charged with indecent exposure and convicted. Now, you won't believe this, the girl in question was walking along the main road, towards Wicklow, near Kilmacanogue, she thumbed a lift and the car stopped. When she entered and sat down, she said that the driver — my client — was not wearing his trousers.'

Of course we laughed. At least this case was unusual.

'Have you anything to go on?' I asked. 'It's difficult to credit such a story.'

'There is something, though it's not very much. Joe McCarroll, my solicitor, cross-examined her, and before he sat down he said: "Did this ever happen to you before?" and the girl said, "It did".' 'You should get him off then surely.' 'I should. Kenneth Deale is a great man for pondering intellectual theories and no doubt he'll think there's something Freudian about this case. Whatever about it happening once, it surely is a most unique experience and could never have happened twice.

'I think if I can give this girl a gentle, but good cross-examination, Kenneth will see that she has a hang-up about this sort of thing and will probably acquit.'

Off he went to Wicklow. I didn't see him for a couple of weeks. When next I met him he was in good form.

'How did that case go?' I asked.

He rubbed his hand across his face and said, 'Oh Jasus, you wouldn't believe how it went.'

'What happened?'

'Well, as you said, it was such an unlikely story that I had very little trouble cross-examining the girl. When I had finished I asked the judge for a direction, saying that I had no case to meet and it would be unsafe to convict on the evidence that he had heard so far.' Kenneth Deale decided cases like this on strict proof and would give an acquittal if there were any sort of reasonable doubt.

'He was puzzled by the whole thing, I could see,' Rex continued, 'and very doubtful about it and I pressed him to say that there must be a lack of proof of the certainty required to convict a man of a sexual offence. Eventually he said, "I agree, but put your client in the box to deny the charge formally, after all the girl has sworn he did what he did and he should repudiate her story."'

'What happened then?'

'Full of confidence I called him into the box,' Rex continued, 'I said to him, "Mr Soames, will you tell me this, on the day of 17 June at Kilmacanogue, were you driving your car?"

'"I was."

'"And were you or were not wearing your trousers?"

'After a long pause, the man said, "To the best of me recollection and to the best of me belief on that day I was wearing me trousers."'

He was convicted.

'What about her story of the experience?' I said to Rex.

'Well, she'd had a similar experience, but not of the same type exactly, although it happened in a car. Such a bloody idiot.'

Later Rex defended a seventy-three-year-old man who was charged with assaulting a girl of eighteen. He was an Irish American and he introduced himself when he was a lodger in her mother's house by saying to her, 'Call me Al.'

It was a jury case. The girl's evidence was pretty convincing, but Rex tried the fatal thing — laughing the case out of court.

'May I remind you', he said, 'of the old adage and eighteenth century nursery rhyme:

> *Between twenty and thirty if a man lives right,*
> *It's once in the morning and twice in the night,*
> *Between thirty and forty, if he still lives right,*
> *He misses a morning and often a night.*
> *Between forty and fifty, it's now and then,*
> *Between fifty and sixty, it's God knows when.*

'And what', continued Rex, 'can it be when you're over seventy years of age? This claim is preposterous. This old man is not capable of even squeezing a girl's knee.'

Whereupon there was a roar from the dock:

'Ya bloody liar, there isn't a woman in the country that'd be safe from me, unless she was wearing tin pants.'

'Be quiet', Deale said to him, very prissily. 'If you wish to communicate with your counsel, you may do so through your solicitor. You cannot be shouting instructions in court.'

'My counsel, he's no counsel, I'm getting rid of him. I'll do the case myself. No man will talk about Al in those terms. I can haul many a fine woman from America to back up what I say.'

Rex changed his method of conducting the case and his client convicted himself.

One of the most irritating things from a judge is constant interruptions. Some judges do it because they are stupid and believe they know more about the case than counsel who are conducting the action. Judges who have not much between the ears write down every word. So busy are they making their notes that they fail to observe the demeanour of witnesses. Craftiness and deviousness go unnoticed just as patent honesty in a witness.

Of a different calibre, however, was Seán Butler, a man of very agile mind, who knew that in each case there is one good point and one or two minor ones. He got on to the point right away. Indeed he sometimes got onto the point before the case started, having read the papers in his chamber before coming into court. His closing addresses to the juries were masterpieces of subtlety, more forceful than the rhetoric of counsel for the injured party.

Seán was a man of extreme kindness and good nature, without the slightest sense of his own importance. Interruptions and a rather strident manner on the bench made him disliked by some.

Anyone who has practised law will know that not until the parties are about to enter the door of the courtroom will they begin to negotiate seriously. Then you ask the judge's usher for about ten minutes to try and settle the case and at the end of that period you would hear kicking on the door giving access to Court No. 1: Seán was becoming impatient. The usher was as terrified as everybody else.

'Ask him for five more minutes.'

'Jasus, I daren't, he's like a greyhound in the trap in there.'

Seán would then come out bellowing at everybody, and the clients would get so frightened that the case would immediately be settled. He would then shout and scream for the next case and the same process might happen again.

Pomposity and long-windedness he hated. Some of my colleagues were noted for this. As he sprang out of his room and mounted the steps to the dais, he once looked down and, seeing two particularly long-winded Senior Counsel, he put his hand up to his face and said, 'Oh Jasus!'

Up to a short time ago the Central Criminal Court used to be burdened with many trivial cases, as anyone could apply for a transfer from the lower court and get it, as of right, whereas nowadays its jurisdiction is confined to murder cases. The accused would size up the judge he was likely to get in the Circuit Court and apply for a transfer. In one such case a man was accused of grievous bodily harm; the individual who was assaulted was none too bright and his evidence was coming in a very unsatisfactory manner.

Seán took over.

'Tell us,' he said, 'what injuries did you sustain?'

'I was bleeding from the head, me eye was black, me nose was deviated and I lost a tooth.'

'I see,' said Seán, 'so you say that you were badly injured.'

'Indeed I was', said the man. 'I suffered terrible and I got a terrible fright.'

'How did you get all this?' asked Seán.

'Sure I got it in the marbles, that's what happened.'

'You got it in the marbles', said Seán, his voice rising.

'That's right, your honour.'

'You're telling me that, as a result of this assault, your head was bleeding, your eyes were black, your nose was deviated and you lost a tooth.'

'That's right.'

'And now you're telling me you got a belt in the marbles.'

'That's right.'

'How could that be?' shouted Seán. 'How could a belt in the marbles produce those injuries?'

It dawned on the plaintiff.

Ah, yer Honour, it's a mistake.'

'I'm sure it's a mistake and you'd better be careful about your evidence if you want to be believed.'

'But sir, yer Honour, I wasn't kicked or hit in those marbles, I got hit in the Marbles Disco.' There was a dance hall in Dublin at that time known as The Marbles.

Michael O'Maolain, defending a man for assaulting his girlfriend, pleading self defence, shouted at the lady in cross-examination.

'And not only did he not hit you, but it was you assaulted him, didn't you give him a dunt in the bollocks?'

'What did you say?' asked the District Justice.

'I said she gave him a dunt in the bollocks.'

'What's that? What does that word mean?' asked the judge.

'Oh, bollocks, well politely, testicles I suppose.'

'I know that, but what does the word "dunt" mean?'

Judge Butler was a man of very temperate habits. I never knew him to take more than a couple of bottles of stout or a gin and tonic. His knowledge of Dublin public houses, however, seemed immense, although he was not a Dublin man. In motor accident cases he identified every scene of collision with reference to public houses. An obscure place in Drumcondra would be identified by reference to Ryan's, Mulligan's, The Fallen Horse or some such

at least 75%. of the cases cited in this book involve violence to women.

hostelry. He had also a remarkable knowledge of things mechanical. I believe he could have built himself a house.

Shortly before he died, a new Silk whom he did not know well appeared in a case. He was a Cork man with a 'fierce' accent. Calling his client to the box, who on being duly sworn was invited to sit down, he told him, 'Speak up now like a good man as loud as you can. Try to emulate me.'

Seán bent down. 'To do that he'd have to attend the Abbey School of Acting', he said.

It is a great pity that Seán Butler did not survive to try actions without the tedium of a jury. As I said, his mind was razor sharp, ahead of everybody else, so his interferences in the conduct of the case became irksome to practitioners who had to plod their way through the evidence for the benefit of the jury, stressing points over and over again to ensure they sank home. Sometimes he answered their questions before they were finished or he supplied witnesses with their responses.

In one such case in which I was concerned, he took a dislike to the plaintiff. She claimed that she was unable to drive a motor car because of a whiplash injury in her neck. The insurance company had employed a private detective, who followed her from her home while she drove her car into the heart of Dublin, parked, shopped and drove back again without any sign of disability. She repeated this practically every day. Consequently, having said in her direct evidence she could not drive, had never driven since her accident, Seán Butler, although generally in favour of plaintiffs, took a dislike to her. She got very little damages.

However, Fred Morris, who was for the injured lady, appealed to the Supreme Court. He pointed out, in opening his case, that out of the eight hundred or so questions asked at the action, over four hundred had been put by the judge. Fred argued that, notwithstanding anything the lady may have said, there was such an unwarranted interference in the trial that the verdict should be set aside. The court agreed and directed a new trial on the basis that it was unsatisfactory for the judge to interfere so much in the combat. The lady was not so befuddled at the next hearing and she got fairly good damages.

Any time I had a case from Dundalk it was usually a hopeless and lost cause. I was handed a brief one afternoon to appear the following day for a man who was claiming damages against his employer. He was a farm labourer. During a hedge slashing job, a thorn entered his finger, he took little notice of this, only when it was extremely painful and oozing did he go to a doctor. To avoid blood poisoning of his whole system, the finger had to be amputated.

My instructing solicitor and I discussed the case. What did the employer do wrong? It was suggested that he should have been supplied with gloves, but no one had ever heard of a farm labourer wearing gloves, nor could the employer be criticised unduly for not taking such a precaution when no other farmer in the whole country did so.

'I have George Edge in the case', said my solicitor.

'Ah!' George was an engineer, primarily a motor engineer, but he gradually became an expert in all sorts of matters mechanical, an expert in systems which should be operated in factories for the safety of the workers. He drew plans, took photographs and gave forceful opinions against neglectful employers.

I seldom saw a man who could bend the evidence so much and thoroughly believe in it. He was in fact a spare time minister in religion and a lay preacher. He was always cheerful and optimistic.

'George Edge,' I said, 'how can he help us?'

'George is going to say that he ought to have been supplied with gloves.'

'What sort of gloves?'

'He has a pair of asbestos gloves which are worn by factory workers. He's going to say that any sensible farmer would give his worker a pair of these things.'

On the morning of the case, I cringed, practically going down on my knees and begging my opponent for a settlement. The insurance people were contemplating a victory and they were there sneering.

'Not even a few hundred pounds for the man himself? No costs for us?'

Nothing.

We drew Seán Butler in Court No. 1.

George gave his evidence. He stuck to his guns. He knew farmers didn't buy these gloves. It wasn't the custom in the country, he conceded, but anyone should anticipate this injury to a workman, some sensible precautions should be taken.

Seán listened patiently enough. At the end of my case he asked, 'What have you got to go to the jury, what evidence?'

'There is evidence — gloves', I said.

'Did you ever in your life see a farm labourer wearing gloves?'

Although I had learnt a great deal about farming practices as a junior working in the country, I could say very little about this, except that Mr Edge had given the evidence.

'Mr Edge! Mr Edge, would give evidence as to the best method of frying eggs on a hot pavement.'

This remark, though true, I disputed by saying that as long as I had been in practice, Mr Edge had given his evidence in every court, having the greatest respect from all judges.

'He's the expert's expert', said Seán.

My opponent, however, forgot the one vital point. He never asked that the case should not go to the jury, to the twelve good men and true, who naturally decided in favour of the plaintiff, giving him the appropriate damages for the loss of his finger.

There was the inevitable appeal to the Supreme Court — gloves for farm labourers!

Over the long vacation I took to Thomas Hardy, reading *The Mayor of Casterbridge,* I was enchanted with the description of a large country town in or about the middle of the last century. The bustling activity, the purchase of farm implements and there, difficult to believe, amongst everything that could be purchased, were strong leather gloves, or gauntlets for the use of hedge trimmers. If they were used in those times where so little heed was paid to the safety of children working in factories, or to men working anywhere, then surely it was not too much to expect that the modern farmer would have heard of them.

I held the verdict in the Supreme Court. Instead of the law cases, I cited Thomas Hardy.

20

I knew one prominent Dublin solicitor whose family were cattle dealers. Before the cattle markets took over the industry and there were cattle dealers all over the country, most of them tended to go to my friend.

As he opened his office one morning, a client was waiting. He could scarcely restrain his indignation and tell his tale of woe until the prominent person sat down. The client had had a dispute with a large farmer in County Meath over the sale of an animal.

It happened, he said, at the fair at Maynooth. The farmer had agreed to sell him a certain prize animal, but afterwards went back on his bargain, an unheard of thing, and he wanted damages for this. His reputation as a cattle dealer was at stake. The money didn't matter, only very little was involved, but this was a matter of principle.

Suppressing a sigh, the solicitor proceeded to write down the particulars of the matter. Horror, his pen poised in the air, he learned that the proposed defendant was a very large land owner, who was also a client of his. He thought quickly.

If he started proceedings against the land owner, he would certainly lose him to another solicitor — for ever. If he were to explain to the cattle dealer that he did not wish to act in the case because of his relationship with the proposed defendant, he reflected gloomily that the cattle dealer would be off to some other rival. If he decided to act for nobody, he was certain that one or other, or both of them would leave. He had both their wills in his safe and all their respective family business came to him.

'All right, Tom', he sighed. 'You have a good case, I'll get going on it. I'll start proceedings for you as soon as I can, but I'll have to write a few letters first of all.'

He did nothing, a few days passed. His client phoned to know had there been any answer to the letters. He thought.

'No, Tom,' he said, 'the letter was not answered, what do you want me to do? Do you want to drop it? After all he is a well-respected man.'

'Well-respected? False respectability. Sue him, I'm the laughing stock of Maynooth already, and I won't show my face there next month if you don't bring him as quickly as you can to court.'

Disputes involving principle can only be resolved by capitulation or defeat of one party by the other. The solicitor had an inspiration. After a day he rang his client.

'Your action will be coming on shortly in the Circuit Court in County Meath. I've issued the Civil Bill, I'll let you know the exact date for the hearing.'

Two weeks later, he wrote to his client:

'Good news for you. Having issued the proceedings on your behalf against Mr Cullen, I received a cheque from him for the full amount claimed, plus my costs, so you can forget all about your unhappy experience. I now enclose that sum and hope that you are satisfied.'

The cattle dealer, though disappointed that he had not his day out in court, was mollified.

The next time he met his enemy was some months later at the fair in Moate.

'Hey, hey, how are you?' he said.

'Ah, sure not too bad, glad to see you, notwithstanding the fact that we had a row the last time we met.'

'Well anyway that's all over.'

'I'm glad it is.'

'So am I and it's good to see that you had common sense.'

'What do you mean?'

'You had common sense and you didn't wait till I bested you at the court in Trim.'

'What court are you talking about?'

'You know, you know damn well. My solicitor has given me the cheque for me damages for that animal you refused to sell me although you had agreed to do so.'

'You must be off your head, man, I gave your solicitor no cheque. Who is he anyway?'

The name was mentioned.

'Be Jasus, he's my solicitor as well. Don't tell me you went to him.'

'I did, and a very good job he did. Got the money out of you, you old skinflint.'

'You, you unspeakable rotten liar, I paid no money.'

If it were in the days of shillelaghs, they would now be raised and blows struck.

Next morning the prominent person had two indignant clients storming at the bastion of his office. He lost both of them.

On the very last day before I took silk I was engaged to defend a slander action. My client was a shopkeeper whose premises were close to a bus stop in a small village near the Curragh Camp. On a day when the rain lashed down and the clouds practically touched the ground, a young woman with a two-year-old child made a small purchase in the shop. Her object was to take shelter there until the local bus arrived.

My client proved to be a fat middle-aged man, not too particular about personal hygiene, as I learned when cooped up with him in a tiny consultation room. He fancied ladies, he told me.

The bus being delayed, the child became restless and started crying. The mother made a second purchase, a packet of biscuits, and the little one cheered up. There was one other man in the shop, buying groceries and awaiting the end of the rain. The lady put the child up on the counter, where he sat contentedly munching. The shopkeeper leaned across and leered at her.

'That's a fine child you have ma'am', he said.

'Thank you.'

'Tell me now, how would you like to have the makings of another?' he said.

Shortly after, the bus came and the mother and child departed.

That evening an indignant husband came to the store. His wife, he said to the shopkeeper, had come home in tears, grossly insulted by the rude remarks which had been made. He demanded that the proprietor come immediately to his house and personally apologise to his wife.

'Ah, damn rubbish!' my client said to him. 'No one would have been insulted by what I said. Sure there's no need to apologise for a bit of a joke and that's all it was.'

'It was no joke,' said the husband, 'it was a dirty offensive remark and I demand an apology.'

A Civil Bill claiming damages for slander duly arrived, signed by my friend and doughty opponent, Colm Condon. It was no longer a joke.

Six months later, in a consultation room in Naas, I questioned my client and I advised him that although the defence of non-actionable, mere vulgar abuse was pleaded, the judge, Kenneth Deale, would not like this case by any means. I advised him to try and settle.

'I'm fighting this woman and this man', he said obstinately. 'I may as well tell you, I'm saying these things to women every day of the week, just for the cod of it, just for a laugh, and none of them ever complain. In fact they all love it. Why, you'd be surprised!'

'There is a strong possibility that after this case your style of conversation will have to undergo a dramatic change', said I.

The case was first on the list. Someone knocked on the door and said to me, 'Mr Condon would like a quick word with you.' Colm Condon was a colleague that never tried to bluff.

'My lady and her husband don't want to go to court', he said. 'They would settle for an apology and costs.' I went back to my client.

'How much would it cost me?' he asked.

I said about £75, and this was a good get out.

'Not at all, not at all, fight, fight. I'll not apologise to that bitch or to any other bitch.' _See N̶S̶u̶ on page 136!_

'They say there was a witness in court, a man who was actually in the shop at the time and heard everything.'

'I know who he is, I know who he is, Jack Gilligan.' He closed one eye and winked. 'He'll be no witness for them, I'll tell you.'

A slander has to be proved to be published. One person may say what he likes to another provided it is not heard by someone else.

Colm opened the case in full flight, described his client as a young lady, of exceptional qualities, mother of a young child, whose only interest was to bring up her offspring, to keep humble, clean and comfortable house for her husband, a carpenter in the army, doing his duty for his country. What did he find one day on coming home from his hard day's work? Instead of the usual tasty dinner, he found his wife almost fainting and in floods of tears.

He described the scene in the shop, the humiliation and hurt were such that the shock of the insulting words remained in her memory still. With courage, she managed to conceal her emotion from the careless brute, who had grossly insulted her in the shop and in the presence of a local man, who no doubt heard it all and would communicate it through the neighbourhood. That the

LAWFUL OCCASIONS

lady's name was defamed in the focal part of all local activity, the only grocery and provision shop in the village, made it worse.

'And let me tell you this, my Lord,' Colm said, 'what is the defence? Mere vulgar abuse. Laughable I say, remarks which can only mean that this lady was likely to be available to any man who asked her. That was the way the question was framed and in no way could such words be merely abusive.'

She gave her evidence, wearing a brimmed hat, a blouse and gloves. All the way home in the bus, tears rolled down her face, she said, everybody was looking at her and she was ashamed and felt unclean. She could never bear to go into that shop again, even passing it on the bus reminded her of the appalling scene. Tears then flowed gently down her cheeks as she recalled the incident.

Deale wrote everything down. How could she be cross-examined?

'Wasn't it all said smilingly and in a jesting manner, a kindly sort of compliment, maybe slightly vulgar?'

'Absolutely not, he was trying it on and making a disgrace of me.'

'But he spoke in a low voice didn't he, he couldn't be heard by anyone?'

'He could, there's a man in court who heard it all and I saw him looking at me and laughing.' She made a fine impression on the judge.

'Come up, Mr Gilligan', said Colm loudly in his fiercest voice. 'This witness is under subpoena, m'Lord', he said, indicating that the man could be hostile.

No statement of his evidence was available. Such witnesses are a problem, as they cannot be cross-examined unless they are proved to be hostile in demeanour and have made a statement that contradicts their testimony in the box. So it was with Mr Gilligan who admitted being in the shop. He remembered a lady there all right, but wouldn't recognise her. He heard nothing, he saw nothing, he was a typical brass monkey. He didn't remember any child, no crying, he was too busy about his own affairs. Having lost his wife's list of messages, he was trying to remember and was too busy to listen to anything.

Colm put it to him that he must obviously remember a child crying, a child eating biscuits. No! He had youngsters at home, but he didn't notice this.

144

I asked the judge for a nonsuit, on the basis that no publication of the defamatory statement had been proved. No one heard the remark and therefore it could not be repeated to anyone. The lady's character would not be denigrated locally, no one could have formed any bad opinion of her. It was not a suggestion of unchastity, but mere vulgar abuse. This was rejected. The judge said it must be presumed that a bystander would have overheard what was said. The words were capable of meaning that the lady was not virtuous and had the character of a woman who could be propositioned by a stranger.

The ultimate disaster for the Lothario of the village near the Curragh was his own evidence. He was an appalling witness, repeating to the judge that most women liked his remarks and screeched with laughter all the time he joked. Colm asked him did he frequently address ladies in the following manner: 'I'd like to see you with your nightie off and me in my red pyjamas'; 'I'm sure you like good tools'; or 'Hammering is good for you'. Were these not his usual abusive words?

These he admitted, all jokes he explained.

'Remarks insulting to ladies and making them ridiculous?' asked Colm.

Kenneth gave a caustic judgment. The defence of vulgar abuse was frivolous. He awarded the maximum that the Circuit Court gave in those days, £600. The equivalent in today's money of about £10,000.

I thought that this would financially ruin my client, having such a little shop and in a small way of business. Until I heard that he, like many others in the region — drapers, publicans, butchers — was the owner of a fine stud farm and had several successful racehorses.

21

After squatting for about three years, I had at last obtained my own seat in the Library which I occupied until I left the Bar in 1986. An old man named Hungerford was my immediate neighbour and next to him was Ashley Powell, who was slightly younger. The son of a Cork clergyman, Ashley was the owner of a rather decrepit Georgian house on ten or twelve acres in Templeogue. Were he alive now and were he to sell it, he could retire to the Bahamas, not that he would want to. Before coming into the Library he milked his cows, forked the hay to the dry stock and fed the pigs and hens. If his feet were wet on arriving by bicycle, he took off his shoes and walked around in his bare feet. Generally he was soaked, as he cycled to Dublin every day.

He had a woolly sort of practice and was rather muddled by things generally. As an example of the appalling life of a junior barrister, he was ill for a couple of weeks and on his return I commiserated with him.

'Not at all,' said he, 'not at all. It was marvellous, I was able to lie in bed and do my work and now I have no solicitors pounding on my door. Everything is clear. The great thing is to get to the bottom of the bag.'

Gardner Budd, afterwards a judge of the Supreme Court, sat opposite. As a junior he had the reputation of never losing a case on the Leinster Circuit. I mentioned to him that I had been told this by a solicitor and he laughed.

'Firstly,' he replied, 'I will tell you that I never started a hopeless case, and secondly, I always settled the bad ones. Consequently, there weren't many I could lose.'

For a time, Ashley practised in the Cork Circuit. He should have done well there and I cannot understand why he left. About a practitioner whom he intensely disliked he told me the following story:

A little Cork city girl had been knocked down by a motor car. Young children cannot give evidence in civil courts unless it can be shown that they know the meaning of an oath. The theology in this case was somewhat dubious and certainly not in conformity with modern ecclesiastical thinking. The judge said:

'What happens you if you tell a lie on the Bible?'

'I go to hell', said the child.

'Swear her', said the judge. Her counsel got up to question her.

'Sheila, do you live near McCurtin Road?'

'He blew no hor-an!' the little girl piped out.

'No, no, don't bother about that just now, just tell me where do you live?'

'He blew no horan.'

'Did you see a motor car?'

'He blew no horan.'

Eventually the judge stopped the case, glaring down at the practitioner, who glared at his solicitor, who in turn glared at the ceiling.

Picture a man with a large red nose, tall with piercing eyes, black jacket and waistcoat and striped trousers, with a gold albert on which hung a little bell, and that was Frank Fitzgibbon. You heard him before you saw him as he walked down the Library stairs, the little bell tinkling. Income Tax was his speciality, but he did other cases as well.

A hay barn had gone on fire in a large County Westmeath estate. Having spread to the stables, the fire caused extensive damage, running into many thousands of pounds. A big case in those days. Although County Councils against whom a claim for malicious damage could be brought, usually maintained that such fires started spontaneously by overheating and internal combustion in the hay, there was clear evidence in this case that two fires had been set. I had settled all the documents necessary to ground the claim; Frank was brought in as a senior to conduct the hearing.

A day or two before the case was due to be listed in Athlone, I went up to Frank's desk, stood there for a minute and coughed diffidently. He looked up.

'Well, sonny?' he said.

I was almost tempted to call him 'sir'. We were expected to call each other by our surnames no matter what the age difference was. Christian names were rarely used in those days except between friends. I couldn't bring myself to say 'Fitzgibbon'.

'Well, sonny, don't just stand there.'

'I'm your junior in a Malicious Injury case next Thursday in Athlone.'

'Ah yes, ah yes,' he said. 'Do you go down there regularly on Circuit?'

'Not to Athlone, I'm just lucky to have got this one.'

'Very well, that's very good. You meet me in here at half past eight on the morning of the case and we'll drive down together.'

We duly drove down and met our solicitor. Afterwards we had a consultation: Frank said to me, immediately before we went into court, 'I want you to help me now, sonny, I want you to take two of the witnesses.'

I began to feel rather pale.

'No need to worry, here's a piece of paper, on top is the name of the witness, and the questions. Ask him what's written out there. That's all you have to do.'

On each of two sheets of paper were written about twenty questions, which I duly asked in the course of the case. The correct answers came out. There was little contest, it was only a question of the amount of damages, and we received a high award with, of course, all sorts of costs.

As we were derobing, I said to him, not venturing to call him Frank and not daring to call him Fitzgibbon, could I have the pleasure of asking him to lunch in the Prince of Wales Hotel.

'Don't worry about that, sonny,' he said, 'you come along with me.'

'But', I objected, 'you've carried all this case, I've done nothing.'

'You've been a great help.'

We got into the car, which was a venerable Wolsey.

'We'll have lunch at 1.15,' he said, 'we'll stop down at Clonmacnoise.'

I was mystified by this. We drove down to that beautiful, placid expanse of water and stopped at a convenient parking place.

'Now, sonny', said Frank. He got out, he opened the boot, out came a hamper, full of the most glorious food and a bottle of good red wine.

This treat was an example of how an Irish picnic should be prepared, and I imitated it all my life. Frank had married a lady whose family owned the famous Zetland Arms Hotel in Cashel,

Connemara. She had prepared this repast. For a while, Frank, Chris Micks and two others actually took over and ran the hotel, but they never made it commercially viable. They also had one of the best sea trout and salmon fisheries in the whole of Ireland.

Like Arthur Chance in the medical profession, Frank was reputed to receive enormous fees for his income tax opinions. This was untrue. His charges were commensurate with his work and in no way beyond what most good Senior Counsel would expect.

He once advised a solicitor in County Cavan on a big income tax matter. Not entirely liking the solicitor who instructed him, he wrote and said his opinion was ready. On receipt of a fee of one hundred guineas, he would send it.

The fee was paid, the opinion merely stated:

'This company should appeal the assessment, it will certainly succeed.'

Indignantly, the solicitor wrote back to know the reasons for Frank's opinion and the authorities upon which he relied.

The answer came: 'The reasons are my own, I will keep them until the hearing of the case.'

Frank told me about this during our journey.

'The damn fellow,' he said, 'once he had the opinion, would be sending it around among all the other solicitors, all of them getting free advice at my expense.'

He was quite right, opinions ought to be in the copyright of counsel. Ownership is with the person who pays for it, but it should not be for circulation. It is an absolutely maddening thing for a barrister to find that his opinion is, if it is on a point of law, being used by solicitors who are strangers to him.

Shortly after that occurrence, I got another good case with Frank. A merchant ship had come into the port of Waterford, had been directed by the Harbour Master to a berth and had tied up. That night there was an exceptionally low tide. The ship was loaded and large. As the tide went out, her keel lay on the bottom where it rested on a large rock. Using nautical parlance, one might say that the strain broke the back of the ship and caused extensive damage.

Amid a morass of case law the situation was perfectly simple. Anybody who goes on business into another's shop or premises doesn't expect to be insured against all risks. It is the duty of the owner or occupier to have the place safe and to protect him who enters from any unusual dangers which either are known to him or ought to be known.

The harbour authorities should have known that the berth was not safe for a large ship, the draught of which was in excess of the footage which would enable it to float in low water. The harbour bottom was dangerous and liable to cause damage.

The instructing solicitor was Ned Fitzgerald, a practitioner of great distinction, with the most melodious speaking voice that I have ever heard.

A consultation had been arranged with the master and the mate and other relevant witnesses. I expected this meeting to last all evening.

Frank came in with his brief. Now the conduct of consultations is most extraordinary. Some people do not know how to get them off the ground. They mumble and they fumble, they leaf through papers, they get all the names wrong, they don't appear to know very much about the case and, in my opinion, some terrible impressions are made at such meetings. Clients lose confidence in their case and in their counsel when they are asked 'What are you going to say in court?'

Not so Frank. He had a little child's copybook in which he had written in pencil a number of questions. He had assumed quite rightly that Ned Fitzgerald had all the information which was required for the case and that the statements had been properly taken. The consultation was over in half an hour. Frank asked his questions, noted the answers of the captain and the mate and said good afternoon.

He opened the case to the judge next day, like an ancient storyteller unfolding a drama. 'The ship steamed from the Port of Bristol to the bay where three great fishing rivers meet'. He came to the crunching noise and the shuddering of the ship: '... and there was that beautiful object damaged, to the horror of the Captain', and, finished with the facts, commenced to read the correspondence. The judge said that he'd not got the letters that Frank was reading in the papers before him.

'I can't understand that', said Frank.

From the back of the court, with a suitcase spilling papers all over the place, Ned Fitzgerald rushed up and said, 'Oh, Frank, Frank, you told me not to include those letters in that particular section.'

'That's all right', said Frank. 'M'Lord,' he addressed the judge, 'my instructing solicitor tells me that the reason you have not got this correspondence is my fault. Like Marshal Joffre, after the Battle of the Marne, when asked who was the author of the victory, said, "I do not know who is responsible for winning the battle, but I do know, if it were lost, it would be me who was to blame." Therefore, like the Marshal, I take the responsibility.'

When these great barristers passed on, a great deal of tradition was lost. Their duty to the court and their duty to the client was the first and foremost thing in their minds. Their incomes were low, the fees were miserably small, even taking into account the cost of living and inflation. What they were paid was in no way commensurate with the earnings of the Bar today. They laboured on without the benefit of modern machines, they worked day and night, there were no pension schemes, the life was precarious indeed.